CHRISTIAN REUNION:
HISTORIC DIVISIONS RECONSIDERED

CHRISTIAN REUNION:

HISTORIC DIVISIONS RECONSIDERED

by

J. S. WHALE

LUTTERWORTH PRESS · LONDON

First published 1971

LONDON

LUTTERWORTH PRESS, 4 BOUVERIE STREET, EC4Y 8BE

ERRATUM

Line 15, page 121 should read:-
to the Catholic Leslie Dewart than he was to the Missouri

For

HELEN and JOHN

ISBN 0 7188 1795 8

Printed in Great Britian by
Ebenezer Baylis and Son Limited
The Trinity Press, Worcester, and London

CONTENTS

PREFACE

WHEN THE MEMORIAL HALL trustees honoured me with their invitation to give the Congregational Lectures, 1970, I felt sure that a theme from the field of historical theology would be welcome, especially if it were related to the widespread contemporary interest in Christian Reunion. The four lectures were accordingly entitled 'The Ecumenical Ideal and the Relevance of Classic Conflicts'. Recalling and facing these divisive theological issues of the past which have enduring relevance, the lectures tried to be realistic as well as ecumenical in temper, and to make a small offering to Christendom's growing fund of catholicity. This book publishes them in the expanded form of six chapters and an epilogue.

Congregational Independency does not forget Robert Browne's pioneering assertion of its first principles, four centuries ago, in his *Treatise of Reformation without Tarying for Anie*. We even remember the two men who were hanged at Bury St. Edmunds for circulating it, and reflect that such strenuous oppressions rarely quench the human spirit: the blood of the martyrs is seed.

But we look forward as well as back. Without committing ourselves impulsively to *Reunion without tarrying for any*, as if this were now the only word which the Spirit is saying to the Churches, we are nevertheless somewhat saddened and ashamed as we reflect on the long history of schism; and we find in the modern ecumenical movement something so unprecedented that we welcome it, and want to reckon responsibly with its implications.

Much has been said in recent years about the non-theological factors in Christendom's historic divisions. I am not unaware of their importance, but this book is not concerned with them. It is concerned, explicitly, with those theological issues which

7

are notorious for their continuing power to separate Christians into rival camps, the nature of the Church, and the nature of the Sacrament which is the focus of its worship and life.

As the title and sub-title of the book may indicate, its chapters fall roughly into three parts.

In the first part, Chapter I tempers ecumenical enthusiasm with history's witness to an element of paradox in all Christian ecclesiology. Successive conceptions of the Church do not escape it, either in the era of the New Testament, the Augustinian era of the Middle Ages, or the reforming era of Protestantism. There is tension at the heart of each; and it is Western Christendom's tragedy that with Protestantism—no more immune from this tension than early or medieval churchmanship had been—there came an irreparable break. Chapter II sets out the theology of this break with Rome in the historic polarity of Mass and Communion Service.

In the second part, the main theme is christology—the great issue which has tended to divide Christians from the beginning, and which is a major clue to theological breaches within Protestantism, notably that between the Lutheran and Reformed traditions over the Real Presence. I shall be encouraged if these two chapters prove acceptable across the Atlantic as a modest English supplement to *Marburg Revisited*, an ecumenical symposium on the same theme by Lutheran and Presbyterian scholars there. (See the bibliography to Chapter IV, p. 96 below.) The pertinence of the theme is clear as soon as we abandon vague generalities and wrestle with precise answers to questions raised by what we say and do at Altar or Lord's Table. The nominal Christian, whose easy tolerance over such questions is hardly distinguishable from indifference, may dismiss 'battles long ago' with ill-concealed impatience; but, as Cardinal Heenan's remark quoted on p. 46 below makes clear, the kingdom of truth may not be taken by violence or indifference, either in the sixteenth or in the twentieth century.

In the third part, however, the passion of past controversies *is* seen in a new light. Chapters V and VI try to take an honest look at the fact, and revolutionary meaning of the 'Modernity' which has been making the 'Past' so largely out-of-date and irrelevant for over a century now. Our historical approach to ecumenical issues thus becomes an appraisal of modern historiography, especially in the field of biblical research. It asks whether the erosion of traditional structures of Christian belief by modern historicism may not have constructive ecumenical import. May not the acids of modernity prove to be healing medicine?

As it would be somewhat pretentious to burden a modest essay of this scope with a mass of footnotes and detailed references to sources, I have eliminated them entirely, in the hope that the bibliography at the close of each chapter may indicate the authorities to which I am most indebted.

ACKNOWLEDGMENTS

I am grateful to Lady Collins for readily allowing me to quote from Dr. J. A. T. Robinson's *But that I can't believe* (Fontana, 1967) in Chapter VI; and to the Society for Promoting Christian Knowledge for the same courtesy regarding the quotation from Professor C. K. Barrett's *Jesus and the Gospel Tradition* (S.P.C.K., 1967) in Chapter VII. That chapter also benefits from the comment on Milton in *God's Englishman* (Weidenfeld and Nicolson, 1970) which I use by kind permission of the Master of Balliol.

In Chapter V, I have used the greater part of the Ryder Smith Memorial Lecture, 'What has Athens to do with Jerusalem?', which I delivered in King's College, London, in October 1966. My warm thanks are due to the Epworth Press, who published it as a pamphlet in 1967, for kindly concurring in this.

September 1970   J. S. W.

UNITY AND UNIFORMITY: THE NATURE
OF THE CHURCH

THE average Christian is so used to schism that he has little sense of its enormity. Accustomed from childhood to a divided Church, he speaks innocently of 'churches'. The billboard on the American highway bids him 'Go to Church Sunday; the Church of your choice'. Ignoring the great New Testament imagery of one flock, one shepherd, one body, one loaf, he prefers a coat of many colours to a seamless robe. Common sense tells him that a monolithic uniformity is neither likely nor desirable.

The modern ecumenical movement is somewhat startling, therefore, because it challenges this complacent acceptance of our unhappy divisions. It is a real movement, which is no longer willing to pay lip-service to an ideal, and to defer reunion to the Greek Kalends: it means business and wants ecumenical action.

But such action, if it is to be responsible and realistic, pre-supposes serious thought about the Church, its Sacraments and its Ministry. The Church as such comes to the forefront of our dogmatic interest. The classic debates of the Christian centuries as to its nature, meaning and structure have a renewed relevance. There are three chapters of Church History which are classic expressions of the enduring ecclesiological problem, and we may fittingly begin by looking at them again.

i

THE FORMATIVE AGE: PENTECOST AND AFTER

First, there is the opening chapter; the birth and early life of the Church to which the New Testament is the main monument. Here Christianity understands itself in terms of three ancient concepts which at long last have been realized. The first was the concept of Spirit: the coming Age of the Messiah would be life in the Spirit with all its supernatural blessings. The second was the concept of Community: life in the Spirit was corporately conceived: Israel's long-awaited Messiah was not thought of as an isolated individual but as one with whom a messianic community would appear and which he, in some sense, would embody. The third was the concept of 'Torah', the holy Law of Israel. As far back as Jeremiah we meet the conviction that in the messianic era the Torah will be spontaneously loved and obeyed by the Spirit-filled community. 'I will put my Law in their inward parts and write it on their hearts.'

The New Testament declares throughout that this threefold eschatological faith is present, experienced fact. The first thing we notice is that Spirit is the inclusive atmosphere of its thought. *The Acts of the Apostles*, for example, is a document pervaded by the sense of its presence and power. Second, the Christian Church is the community of the Spirit; the sign and proof of the presence of the New Age, the Kingdom of God. Christians are the fellowship of those who are already tasting of its powers. Third, the Law is now fulfilled as the Law of Christ. The indwelling Christ replaces the Torah written on tables of stone at Sinai: He is the new Torah written inwardly on the tables of the heart.

What is Pentecost but a dramatization of this New Testament witness? Luke's primary purpose in his story of rushing wind, tongues of fire and intelligible foreign languages is interpretation. He is not so much a chronicler here as an artist; and the clue to his picture comes from two ancient legends; one about Babel; the other about Sinai.

Pentecost is to be interpreted, first, as *Babel Reversed*. Legend had it that once upon a time men spoke but one language. In their anxious pride they resolved to build a tower as high as heaven: 'Glory to man in the highest'. Whereupon the Lord punished their presumption by confusing their language and making them unintelligible to one another. The divisions and estrangements of history are the result. But Jewish tradition knew of an evangelical epilogue to this grim legend of judgment. In the fulness of time God will reverse man's predicament: the barriers which make community impossible will be done away: 'Ye shall become one people of the Lord and one tongue'.

Luke is saying, then, that Pentecost saw the reversal of Babel; the fulfilment of the apocalyptic hope, not only for Israel but for all mankind. The misdirection of all human life, of which Babel is the symbol, is now being met by the redeeming action of God in Christ, of which Pentecost is the symbol. In the fellowship of the Spirit man's immemorial alienations are at an end. Thus the birthday of the Church has ecumenical meaning: its mission is world-wide. This is Good News, Gospel.

In the second place, Pentecost is here interpreted as *Sinai Fulfilled*. An ancient festival of harvest, it was also the traditional anniversary of the giving of the Law on Sinai; Israel's greatest historic moment; the effective sign of her deliverance from bondage; her sublimest covenant experience. Wonders had marked this giving of the Law long ago; a Voice from heaven and Fire. Tradition had elaborated this, too. The divine Voice divided into seven Voices; then into seventy tongues, that all peoples of the earth might hear and understand each in their own tongue. This, of course, is *midrash*, legend. But the evangelist is recalling it as he links the first Whit Sunday with the supreme moment of Israel's past. For it is the heart of the New Testament gospel that in the fact of Christ the meaning of God's covenant with his people at Sinai is finally realized. It is universalized. His Church, the Community of the Spirit, fulfils Israel's age-long eschatological hope. Here he makes all things new. Here is new Creation, new Exodus, new Covenant, new Law, new Israel, new Age, new Man, the new Jerusalem coming down out of heaven from God. The Church is the place of his glory, his holy Bride, his Body.

(a) Ecclesiology and Paradox

But is this glowing picture convincing? Do the mundane facts corroborate its high transcendental imagery? The answer must be No as well as Yes: that paradox to which the opening chapter of church history bears candid witness, and which writes itself ineffaceably into every subsequent chapter. Here in this heroic age of Christian beginnings this enduring paradox has two main aspects.

First, it is paradoxical that the end of the old era, which is already here, is not yet here. Even in the new Jerusalem the old Adam is still discernible: the pathetic fraud of Ananias and Sapphira; party-slogans, strife and divisions at Corinth, not to mention a case of incest: the Church in Ephesus has left its first love: Laodicea is only lukewarm: all very human and familiar. In short, though Jesus is already crowned with glory and honour, not yet do we see all things put under him. The experience of the early Christians is tense with this antinomy of 'already' and 'not yet'. The great gifts of God in the new age are present possessions, yet objects of hope.

Our paradox has a second aspect. Early church history says Yes and No to the community of the Spirit in another way. Speaking with tongues, ecstatic prophesyings, varying forms of spiritual experience, are still the accepted mark of the Church in the early years of the second century. A typical man of the Spirit is the wandering prophet, making his inspired random pronouncements uncontrolled by external criteria: enjoying, and sometimes exploiting, the reverence due to his charisma. Even in the first century, therefore, the Church begins to protect itself against extravagances. Spirit which is by definition the constitutive reality of the Church becomes, in experience, a growing embarrassment and menace to the Church. What do you do when questionable claims are made in the name of the unquestionable axiom? In the earliest document of the New Testament (1 Thessalonians) we read 'Don't snuff out the Spirit's flame. Don't belittle prophesyings. But test everything.' And this anticipates more explicit mis-givings and warnings: 'Don't trust every Spirit. Test them whether they be of God. There are many false Spirits'. Paul's great hymn to love tells the Corinthians: 'As for prophets, their work will be over; and tongues of ecstasy? they will cease'. This means that with the expansion of the Church comes its necessary consolidation. It has to be organized. The first rapture of missionary zeal cannot do without definitions and decisions: it cannot do without officials. We see the beginnings of this in those spuriously Pauline documents, the Pastoral epistles. Liturgy tells a similar story. To pass from *I Clement*, the *Didache* and Justin Martyr in this formative period to Cyril's *Catecheses* and the so-called *Apostolic Constitutions* in the fourth century, is to pass from free prayer and exhortation to fixed liturgical formulae allowing nothing to individual arbitrariness or the hazards of improvisation. Tension is already discernible between ardour and order; between spontaneity and authoritative form. The expanding Church is both frightened and fascinated by Gnosticism, that widespread medley of speculative theosophies and redemption cults. When the glorious liberty of the children of God becomes the licence of gnosticizing phantasy, an appeal to the faith once delivered to the saints is not surprising. By the middle of the second century credal orthodoxy, an authoritative canon of scripture and a ruling episcopate will be generally accepted; and not as strait-waistcoat but as trustworthy armour. Early in that century, indeed, Ignatius, Bishop of Antioch, urges the indispensability of the local bishop in almost every letter he writes. At the risk of threshing straw, I quote: 'Christians must regard the bishop as they regard the Lord himself.' 'Apart from the bishop and his clergy the word "Church" is a misnomer.' 'To baptize or celebrate apart from him is to serve the devil.' 'To honour the bishop is to honour God.'

(b) The meaning of Hierarchy

These shrill pronouncements have delighted Anglo-Catholics and made Free Churchmen see red; but their historic meaning is that if Christ is not to fade into a cult god, his Church being lost in some syncretistic mummery, order is vital. The local bishop is its local expression and guarantee. In the declining Empire cities and municipalities sink slowly into apathy, whereas the *ecclesiae* will keep their vitality thanks to their proper episcopal shape. We need not go to the caricatures of a Lucian or a Celsus to see why the wind of the Spirit is no longer deemed to blow as it lists. The Spirit certainly dwells in each individual Christian, incorporating him through baptism into the one Body; but this is now being canalized. The classic thesis 'where the Spirit is, there is the Church' is not repudiated, of course: but it is replaced in fact by the new thesis 'where the Bishop is, there is the Church'. By A.D. 180 Irenaeus, the first systematic theologian, declares the bishops to be the supreme repository of true charisma (*charisma certum veritatis*). Spirit now operates sacramentally through given authoritative forms. The ecumenical meaning of Pentecost is conveyed only through the hierarchy of the Catholic Church.

Seventy years later this is momentously developed by Cyprian, Bishop of Carthage, that transitional figure in whom the Christianity of the sub-apostolic age is seen changing into the sacerdotal Catholicism of the Middle Ages. To Ignatius the bishop had been the centre of Christian unity in each locality. To Irenaeus he was the depository of apostolic tradition. But to Cyprian he is 'the absolute vicegerent of Christ in things spiritual ... exclusively the representative of God to the congregation, and hardly, if at all, the representative of the congregation before God'.

Cyprian's indubitably low view of the congregation grows out of his high view of its ruling head. The Church exists only so far as it inheres in this divinely appointed and inspired office. The episcopate is the primary condition, the very foundation of the Church. Unity demands it; therefore it is so. 'Never,' wrote one of my revered teachers at Oxford, Vernon Bartlet, 'never was a theory less historical.' But the theory triumphed. For as the larger churches in the imperial cities developed dioceses on the analogy of imperial administration, this same temper of hierarchical absolutism went on to find an exclusive divine sanction, first for metropolitans and then for the medieval papacy. Christian unity is so identified with the uniformity of clerical organization as to make the latter the exclusive guarantee and only channel of divine grace. This has been the basis of Catholic ecclesiology ever since. Karl Rahner recently reaffirmed it as 'the unalterable divine constitution of the Church'.

In this first formative period, then, ecclesiology begins as a circle with a single centre. It develops into an ellipse with two focal centres, two fields of force in tension. It ends as a circle with a new centre.

THE MIDDLE AGE: AUGUSTINE'S TWO VOICES

We come to our second chapter of history at the opening of the Middle Ages. The Donatist controversy is a second classic presentation of the recurring ecclesiological debate. The great controversialist here was Augustine. He was the first Christian in history—the date is A.D. 400—to make the Church as such the subject of systematic thought.

The Donatist schism began long before he was born, of course—at Carthage in 311, when the last persecution of the Church by the Roman Empire was ending, and the Emperor Constantine was about to make Christianity the established religion of the State. Caecilian had just been consecrated as the new bishop of Carthage by Felix, bishop of Aptungi, on the initiative of the more lax of the two parties in the North African church, and without the concurrence of the stricter party, which was puritan in temper and more proletarian in its sympathies. Led by Donatus, the latter party of over seventy Numidian bishops objected. They believed that Felix had delivered up the sacred books of the Church to the imperial officers in the recent persecution, and that he was therefore one of the 'lapsed' who had cut himself off from the Church. In their eyes he was no bishop and had no power to confer valid orders: his consecration of Caecilian was therefore invalid. Though this belief was soon shown to be false they deposed him and consecrated another in his place. It was the beginning of a schism which, aggravated by several 'non-theological factors', became war of appalling savagery; and dragged on through three centuries until the triumph of Islam liquidated North African Christianity altogether.

The initial issue was whether sacraments duly administered by unworthy ministrants are valid. Here the Donatists, like that earlier bishop of Carthage, the great Cyprian himself, were now out of date and wrong. The validity of a sacramental act cannot depend on the moral worth of the person performing it, or there would be no sacraments at all. No one is *good* enough to baptize, to preach or to ordain. A sacrament duly celebrated has a validity which is unaffected by the character of the celebrant. It is obviously scandalous if the man of God be a bad man; but the relevant comment is St. Paul's: 'Some preach Christ for vainglory and some for contention: nevertheless Christ is preached'. We should note, however, that Christianity has not always been consistent on this point. When the reforming movement was under way in the eleventh century and Gregory VII was imposing celibacy on the clergy, it was argued that validity of orders depended on conduct. But as the principle of forfeiture of orders by sin is essentially fatal to the whole hierarchical system, such 'Donatist' tendencies have been the exception rather than the rule.

The real and enduring issue was the nature of the Church. It is one and holy by definition: *una sancta*. But on which word is the emphasis ultimately to be placed? The Donatist position was expressed by a verse from Psalm 140: 'Let not the oil of the sinner come upon my head'. The answering slogan from the rest of Christendom was a verse from the *Song of Songs* 6: 'I have but one dove, one darling'. The fundamental issue, however, was not simply Catholic unity *v.* Puritan separatism, as these texts might suggest; for each side believed in the Church as one and holy, and each claimed to be its exclusive Catholic representative. Christians throughout the world did not belittle holiness (even if they did not practise it!); and it was undeniable that these dissentient Christians in North Africa had the requisite marks of catholicity. For if validity really does depend on criteria such as credal orthodoxy and unbroken episcopal succession from the Apostles, the Donatists could not be faulted. They had all this. They were not heretics nor were their sacraments invalid.

It was at this point in the intermittent battle, now in its ninetieth year, that Augustine entered it. 'Yes', he said, in effect, 'you have the accepted marks of catholicity, but your possession of catholicity in this correct sense doesn't make it an effective possession. Your baptisms, eucharists and ordinations are valid sacramentally but useless spiritually. You do have the means of grace, but not their saving efficacy, since that exists only in the Catholic Church with which you are no longer in communion. Only in the Church, spread in unity throughout the world, does the Holy Spirit operate as the spirit of charity and peace.'

(We may observe in passing that this statement seems a dangerously double-edged weapon for the holy Church throughout all the world to use when it had itself been torn by intrigue and dissensions, anathemas and counter-anathemas, mob-violence and banishments for the past seventy years. But as Donatist savagery did not lag behind that of the fanatical crowds in Alexandria and Antioch, and as there is little to choose between 'Circumcellions' in North Africa and 'Blues and Greens' in Constantinople, we had better ignore the nasty realities common to both sides and return to the nice discriminations of theology. Much theology has this escapist function.)

Augustine is here trying to make a hard distinction. He is admitting that the Holy Spirit operates in schismatic sacraments, but denying that the operation is effective. Only in the Catholic Church is validity effective validity. Such a distinction verges on the absurd. It redefines a hair in order to split it. If 'validity' means that God the Holy Spirit is acting, it seems meaningless (and worse!) to add that his action is nevertheless ineffective. This is the pertinent objection which the Anglican makes to the Roman; which the Presbyterian makes to the Anglican; and which the Quaker could make to the Presbyterian if he were interested in these pathetic categories of inclusion and exclusion. In my own lifetime Pope Leo XIII issued the bull *Apostolicae Curae* which pronounced Anglican orders to be absolutely null and utterly void (*pronuntiamus et declaramus ordinationes ritu anglicano actas irritas prorsus fuisse et esse omninoque nullas*). This meant, as Bishop F. R. Barry put it recently, that '*ecclesia anglicana* is a bogus church, dispensing make-believe and illusory sacraments, through unordained men masquerading as priests. . . . We dare not forget that Anglicans were saying that kind of thing about Methodism and even the Church of Scotland' (*New Christian*, July 25, 1968).

Despite his hair-splitting, then, it is a nice point whether Augustine escaped inconsistency here. He found it difficult to maintain this subtle distinction between the *spiritus sanctus* (the agent in every valid sacrament) and the *spiritus caritatis* (which

19

alone makes the valid sacrament a means of grace). Can one distinguish between objective and subjective validity? If the noun means what it says are not both adjectives irrelevant? We can, perhaps, more easily receive Augustine's similar distinction between *habere* and *utiliter habere* ('to have' and 'to have profitably'). It is the distinction made by Alexander of Hales in the thirteenth century between *gratia gratis data* (grace freely given) and *gratia gratum faciens* (grace making its recipient gracious; i.e. grace being really effective). In short, this differentiation between the real and the effectively real is a distinction between a valid sacramental act and its benefit to the soul; and Augustine says that the former can exist outside the Church Catholic, the latter only within it. He puts this with classic intransigeance in his anti-Donatist treatise on baptism: *Salus extra ecclesiam non est* (there is no salvation outside the Church). This brings us to two talking-points.

(i) First, as in the early Church, there is paradox here, that constant mark of all ecclesiology. Augustine is unambiguously Catholic in the full medieval sense; at the same time, however, he vindicates one of Protestantism's distinctive insights. He is saying in the very words of Cyprian that there is no salvation outside the Church: yet he is at the same time with Luther, subordinating the institutional to the spiritual reality of the Church. Catholic presuppositions as to order and structure are being judged by an earlier and more precious touchstone, the unity of the Spirit in the bond of peace. Here the great Bishop of Hippo is nearer to 1 Cor. 13 and to Pentecost than he is to those letters sent to Trallians and Smyrneans by Ignatius, Bishop of Antioch.

A vital question emerges here: where is this 'Church' which Augustine is discussing? How is it to be identified? The question arises out of an obvious difficulty. Here are two warring Catholicisms, each unchurching the other and each claiming to be the entire Church. Nor is this some negligible historical rarity. Catholic Christendom has rarely been without this problem of schismatic rupture, as the Nestorian, Coptic and other breakaway-movements show: indeed, the huge schism of its Latin West and Greek East has been bitter and continuous for some nine hundred years.

Strife and divisions being characteristic of Catholicism, then, as well as of Protestantism, Christendom cannot evade the question: *Ubi Ecclesia?* By Augustine's day the Bishop of Rome has become increasingly sure that he knows the answer to it, and he is saying so. Indeed, a famous epigram, falsely attributed to Augustine, does this for him: *Roma locuta est; causa finita est* (Rome has spoken; the matter is settled). But what Augustine actually said was different. He was not so explicitly obliging to papal apologists. In the seventy-five chapters of his anti-Donatist treatise *On the Unity of the Church* there is not a single reference to the Roman See as the divinely ordained centre of Christian unity, or to Rome's petrine claim.

Are we reduced to head-counting, then, for the answer to our question: Where is the Church?: the common-sense arithmetic of a majority versus a minority? Admittedly, sheer weight of numbers has some validity even though universality is no necessary test of truth. The Donatist bishop, Tichonius, a scholar and a 'moderate', himself admitted that the excommunication of the rest of Christendom by one North African province—though possible and justifiable in principle—ran the obvious danger of being absurd in fact. But Augustine is far from saying simply that the majority is always right: after all, the memory of Athanasius '*contra mundum*' would prevent his saying that. He doesn't count heads. He condemns schism as such. Schismatics, he says, always allege some sacrilege of others as their justification, whereas schism itself is the great sacrilege. 'There is no just necessity for cutting up the unity ... God never orders schism.' In his notable thirty-third chapter he argues that God's separation of the Ten tribes from the Two involved political, not religious, schism: Elijah and the faithful seven thousand among the Ten are evidence of this.

The argument reaches its climax in the famous words quoted memorably by Newman in the *Apologia*, 'It is the sure judgment of the whole world (*securus judicat orbis terrarum*) that they are not good who cut themselves off from the whole world'. The guilty have now been specified. To offend against the unity of the Spirit by an act of schism is a greater evil than any against which it is a protest. 'Here', wrote Cardinal

Wiseman in 1829, 'the great Augustine was condemning Anglicans in advance.'

(ii) Just here, however, comes our second paradoxical talking-point. Augustine says something else in answer to our question, 'Where is the Church?' Cardinal Wiseman did not mention it. Its key word is 'predestination', which Augustine gets from his great precursor and master St. Paul, and which he hands on to his great disciple John Calvin.

For fifteen centuries theology has been baffled by a two-sidedness in Augustine; a complex of opposites which is not logically resolvable. What was already an embarrassment to his Catholic contemporaries Vincent of Lerins and John Cassian in the fifth century, is still an absorbing enigma to his Protestant successors Loofs and Karl Holl, Nygren and Karl Barth in the twentieth. Two-sidedness.

On the one side, the Church is a visible society; an identifiable homogeneous Institution, girdling the world as a unity; its hierarchical structure prescribed by God himself; the only channel of his redeeming grace; the one ark above the flood.

On the other side, the Church is invisible, save to the eyes of God alone; the company of his Elect; the unknown number of the Predestined; the unpredictable monuments of his sovereign and irresistible grace. It is this double-sidedness which makes the great Augustine the most complex figure in the long history of Christian doctrine.

As churchman, he links Cyprian with Hildebrand, Innocent III and Bellarmine in an undeviating line of ecclesiastical absolutism: hammering heretics, persecuting these Donatist schismatics to the death by calling in the sword of the 'secular arm' against them, his scriptural sanction being Luke 14: 23, 'Compel them to come in'. This spokesman for the Church as an Institution conterminous with the great globe itself is blinded by the false political analogies of Empire: he interprets the unity for which Christ prayed as uniformity; something to be imposed by force upon reluctant minorities; the force of Christianity's late persecutor, the State. Augustine approves of the savageries of the Theodosian Code against heretics. His bitter phrase for the refusal of the Emperor Constantine to persecute unorthodoxy is *ignominiosissima indulgentia* (most dishonourable clemency). And with his doctrine that the Church, by divine right, may require the State to protect and spread the correct ecclesiastical ideology and to liquidate deviationists, he eats his own words about the spirit of charity (*spiritus caritatis*), and sanctions in advance Albigensian crusade and Inquisition.

And yet this churchman is also the great doctor of grace for whom, in the final issue, the Church cannot be defined and identified in any structural, constitutional or legal fashion. *Ubi Ecclesia?* The question recedes and dissolves in the inscrutable depths of the divine election. 'All is of God.' 'Many are called but few are chosen.' The awful potter-pot imagery of Romans 9. Systematized by Augustine and Calvin with pitiless logic, this religious percept becomes a metaphysical concept fatal not only to hierarchical and sacerdotal, but also to all ecclesiastical pretensions and arrogances: indeed, to all human assumptions of superiority.

It is because the Augustinian doctrine of original sin is so great a leveller that the haughty Duchess of Buckingham wrote as she did to Selina, Countess of Huntingdon: 'I thank your ladyship for the information concerning the Methodist preachers. Their doctrines are most repulsive and strongly tinctured with impertinence and disrespect towards their superiors. It is monstrous to be told that you have a heart as sinful as the common wretches that crawl the earth. I cannot but wonder that your ladyship should relish any sentiments so much at variance with high rank and good peerage.'

Augustine never resolves this antinomy of a Church which is both visible and invisible. For him, as for Calvin, God's sovereign grace presupposes all the institutions of the Church as its necessary means. Election is the kernel; but the husk, too, is God-given. Again, like Calvin, he is peremptory in rejecting the logical criticism that predestination is determinism, and election an encouragement to moral laxity. And history vindicates them. For the distinctive feature of the Augustinian–Calvinist–Jansenist tradition has been its puritanism. The researches of Bousset and Hahn have shown the unconscious love-hate relation between Augustine and the Donatist puritanism which he is fighting. He was unwittingly influenced by Tichonius. Indeed, Augustine was subconsciously aware that the Donatist call for conversion and holiness was right; just as he was consciously aware that the majority within the embrace of the Church were neither converted nor holy. His comment on Ps. 36:6 is that there are depths as well as heights in the Church. The good, like mountains, are relatively few: the evil (*male viventes*) are like the great deep. Job, the great outsider from Idumea, is for Augustine the notable type of the elect; for he reminds the empirical Church as it strides the centuries that 'according to the hidden predestination of God there are many sheep outside and many wolves inside'. As Lavengro's Man in Black said about Dante, 'That poem of his cuts both ways'.

In the thousand years of medievalism, then, dominated by the genius of Augustine, ecclesiology is a circle firmly drawn. It is nevertheless an ellipse transcending human delineation: focused not only in the visible means of grace but also in the depth of an eternal decree which is known only to God.

iii

Reformation and its dilemmas

With the Reformation we come to a third momentous chapter of Church history. As its divisive issues are our concern throughout the greater part of this book, a broad summary must suffice to place it in perspective here. (The writer's *Protestant Tradition* offers a more extended and detailed survey.)

Reformation involved a tragic break, largely because it challenged the assumption which still constitutes a fundamental difference between Catholic and Protestant ecclesiology; namely that the Church of Rome is not subject to error; its inherent characteristic is the expression of eternal truth. Professor Rupp has recently observed that the noisy disputant against reform, John Eck, was telling Wittenberg theologians in 1518 that 'properly speaking, the Church cannot be penitent' because, as the Body of Christ, it is sinless.

The Reformers repudiated just that presupposition. But before coming to their momentous attempt to revive the heroic age of Christian beginnings and to recover the fellowship of the Spirit at Pentecost, we should notice that though it was perverse as polemic, Eck's statement was not out of line with Catholicism's essential claim. An absurd abuse rather than a proper use of that claim, it may nevertheless remind us that Catholicism has always been unwilling to admit that the treasure of divine grace is mediated to men in really earthen vessels. The human, finite, and fallible vehicles of that grace must be transmuted in some way. In its Two-Natures christology, for example, the Saviour's humanity is not allowed to be full and complete: it is impersonal: his personality is centred in the divine nature. Again, in the theology of the Mass the bread on the altar is not admitted to be bakehouse bread: it is mysteriously transubstantiated. Holy Mother Church, too, is not in essence what it may seem empirically to be. Catholic ecclesiology tends in fact to be monophysite (i.e. having *one* nature, which is exclusively divine) despite the correct christology of Two Natures which it professes. The Church, therefore, is more and other than the aggregate of fallible individuals composing it: it is suprapersonal and transcends time. It is a *corpus mysticum* preserving its immaculate identity through all the chances and changes of this mortal life. Catholicism declares with Plato that the Universal is the real; not the Particulars. The Church is Dryden's milk-white hind

> Without unspotted, innocent within,
> She feared no danger for she knew no sin.

It would be charitable to suppose that Eck was thinking of this transcendentalized Ideal rather than of the Borgias or of the pathetic Tetzel.

The Reformers were not unmindful of this dimension of the Heavenly. They had read and pondered Ephesians. But with the New Testament in their hands, their thought of the Church was also down-to-earth. The Church on earth is the community or fellowship of those who, despite their sin and failure, are 'in Christ'.

For Rome, priesthood and hierarchy being essential to and constitutive of the Church, the community had but a limited importance. Mass, for example, could be said privately, no congregation being present.

For Protestantism, the community of believers is the constitutive essence of the Church; its *sine qua non*. The faith, worship and life of the Church are meaningless without the *societas fidelium*, a fellowship of those who are gathered in the Spirit and united by love. Individually one with Christ, they are what the New Testament calls 'the Brotherhood'. To use Luther's image of the 'cake' (which, unknown to him, the unknown author of the *Didache* had used fourteen centuries before) the fellowship of the Spirit makes them *'ein Kuchen'*. Here, too, it will be charity on the part of Catholics to remember that Protestantism falls far short of this Ideal in practice.

Despite his later disillusionments, dilemmas and inconsistencies, this was Luther's basic and lasting conception of the Church. Its reality is spiritual. It is the fellowship of all upon earth who believe in Christ and are justified by grace alone through faith. As spiritual and 'invisible', it conceals high mystery; *es ist ein hoch, tief, verborgen Ding, die Kirche*. It is *communio sanctorum*, its members being saints and priests in the spiritual sense which is declared and interpreted in the New Testament. It is the Bride of Christ: the praises of Mary are really the praises of the Church.

Reformation so conceived had two immediate results. Positively, it gave a new and paramount authority to Scripture as the basis and protective roof of the emerging evangelical structure. Negatively, it meant a widespread repudiation of tradition. Institutional and liturgical forms which had been deemed integral to the life of the Church since the days of Irenaeus and Tertullian would have but relative worth and authority thenceforward. The equation of divine law with Canon Law would no longer be accepted as necessarily valid. In short, the fellowship of the Spirit would find its unity not in traditional magnitudes or institutional forms, however sacrosanct. All Protestant ecclesiology begins and ends with the Lordship of Christ, which is direct and immediate, and requires no sacerdotal mediation. All Christians are priests. The Crown Rights of the Redeemer disallow the traditional

26

claims of a mediating priesthood. Hierarchy is a matter of secondary or, ultimately, of no importance. The claim of the Bishop of Rome to rule the Church as Christ's Vicar is repudiated. In short, this attempt to recover the Christianity of the New Testament meant the widespread collapse of an ecclesiology which had been dominant for thirteen centuries.

But, once again, ecclesiology presents us with its recurrent paradox. Protestantism was not ruinous individualism, the *Una Sancta* being dissolved into its component elect atoms. The invisible Church is also visible in the obvious sense dictated by practical necessities. Though Luther trusted to the Word as the self-authenticating and effective reality of the ongoing life of the Church, he spent his reforming life fighting the 'Spirituals' on his left as bitterly as he fought against Rome on his right. (They had presumed to take too logically his own principle of 'the liberty of the Christian man'!) As a sound theologian Luther knew that outward forms are indispensable: they are the God-given bearers of the inward and spiritual Word. Like soul and body in man, the 'inward' and the 'outward', though distinguishable, are not separable. The expression of the 'inward' through the 'outward' is a sacramental principle of God's own ordinance (cf. p. 48 below).

In short, reformers in revolt against forms of ecclesiastical legalism in the name of Pauline liberty were thus made aware of our inescapable paradox: they had to enforce their own forms. Classic Protestantism provides two familiar illustrations of this dilemma.

(a) New presbyter as old priest

The new community-life of the Evangelical Christendom which was now emerging and expanding had, of necessity, to create new modes of organization and new patterns of public worship if things were to be done decently and in order. The priesthood of all believers, for example, becomes a sentimental slogan for anarchy if Protestantism forgets Luther's sane observation: 'all Christians are Priests: true: but they are not all parsons' (*es ist wahr alle Christen sind Priester, aber nicht alle Pfarrer*). It is in the interests of fitness and order that the local congregation or community transfers to certain qualified

27

individuals the preaching of the Word and the celebration of the Sacraments. Such persons receive no special sacral status or indelible character, but a *Dienst und Ampt* (a Ministry and special function). All Christians are Priests as the Minister is; but he, for the nonce, is the mouth of the Community. This is the meaning of Ordination; not, as is claimed for a clerical hierarchy, that it is something 'sacramental'.

Let it not be inferred from this that Luther failed to exalt the Ministry of the Word and the Sacraments. 'Christianity's highest office', he says, 'is laid on the man on whom the preaching office is laid.' As God's instrument the Minister of the Word gives effect to the miracle of grace. Calvin speaks of the *Ministerium Verbi Divini* in the same high strain. Indeed, it is Calvin—reformer of the second generation, greatest of biblical theologians and a Prince of the Church—whose ecclesiastical statesmanship is its own testimony to our immediate theme. Perhaps the successive editions of his *Institutio* best illustrate the paradoxical tensions within the emerging ecclesiology of the early Reformation period.

Primarily he conceives of the Church as the invisible company of the elect, beyond the possibility of human definition. This is his heritage from Augustine. But he goes on to conceive of the Church, also, as the visible body of believers recognizable by their corporate participation in the preached and heard Word, and in the Sacraments. Given the abiding imperfection of the Christian life under grace, no test or touchstone other than this is available. This owed something, doubtless, to Luther. But Calvin goes further. As a zealous steward of Christ's holy law he cannot but think of the Church, too, in terms of that Christian perfection which demands discipline—and inflicts excommunication in the last resort—in the interest of the holiness without which no man shall see the Lord. In short, there is a tense synthesis here, of predestinarian logic, practical churchmanship and puritan perfectionism. The parallel between Calvin and Augustine, new presbyter and old priest, is writ large. Milton hits the nail precisely on the head.

The momentous turning-points in Christian ecclesiology always confirm the old and painful fact that what the Church is in terms of high theory and what it is empirically are very different. Ideally the Church is made up of dedicated spirits as on the day of Pentecost itself. In fact, on that day and ever since this has not been so. As Dodd once observed, pristine perfection is an illusion. In every age, therefore, the ecclesiological issue becomes a practical and a pastoral issue. (This book suggests seriously that in *our* age it becomes the ecumenical issue.) Granted that the Church is the great society outside which there is, in principle, no salvation, must it be understood in terms of holiness—the initial *raison d'être* of Montanists, Donatists, Cathari, Anabaptists, Separatists, Puritans, Methodists and zealous movements innumerable? Or must it be accepted as *Volkskirche* (sometimes Englished as 'C. of E.'), where too absolute a standard for wayfaring men is wisely avoided? The danger in *each* contention is writ so large in history that the modern ecumenical movement is neither sentimental nor lazy in preferring 'a more excellent way' to the recurring pattern of 'strife and divisions'. After all, precedent for this is indisputably old (1 Cor. 3: 3 and 12: 31). This brings us to the second illustration of Protestantism's dilemma.

(b) Evangelical liberty as national establishment

Lord Acton saw the historical importance of Luther's brilliance as a writer. His weighty and powerful manifestoes made history, partly because the man himself was hugely human. In the field of ecclesiology this religious genius was no academic purist. He thought of the Church not only as the invisible community of the 'saints', but as society itself—his own regional and territorial German society for example—in its wayfaring, workaday aspect. He saw that the Church of the people is always richly and pathetically commonplace. Indeed, as an Evangelical Christendom came into being throughout Northern Europe, its leaders found themselves compelled to take up some positive attitude towards the average man: man in the mass. The ecclesiastical statesman's problem was much the same in the Protestant era as in previous eras. He had to concede that the Church in the wilderness of this world is for the whole mixed multitude (Augustine's *corpus permixtum*) and not exclusively for the solemn troops and sweet societies of the elect. Luther, Zwingli, Calvin, More and Cranmer (to name only these) turned against the too zealous 'Spirituals' and Anabaptists, just as Queen Elizabeth I and Whitgift were to turn against the tiresome Puritans.

This establishment and control of religion by the State in the Protestant world of the sixteenth century is usually labelled 'Erastian', because it was advocated by Erastus, a Heidelberg physician of that period. His motive was probably less 'totalitarian' than it sounds, for he felt that victims of tyrannous Calvinist excommunication (with its serious social consequences) should have the right of protection by the secular power of which they were subjects.

But Erastianism, as a generic term for this type of solution of the problem of 'Church and State', may not be limited to the sixteenth century or to Protestantism. Just as Talleyrand was appointing bishops in France over two centuries later, so the territorial princes of Germany had been anticipating Henry VIII and Elizabeth I in their control of the Church in Bavaria and Brandenburg, a hundred years or so before Luther was born. A controlling link between local organs of public law, such as City Councils, and the local Church was becoming common in the later Middle Ages. *L'Eglise au pouvoir des laiques* is the phrase used by the Catholic historian, Augustin Fliche, for a recurrent medieval phenomenon: there was Erastianism even in the 'age of faith'. Luther's appeal to the 'Christian Nobility of the German Nation' was no great novelty therefore. What was his motive? Or, rather, how is Lutheran 'erastianism' to be accounted for? A much discussed problem.

Luther's dilemma, from 1522 onwards, is his fight on two fronts. Opposing Rome on his right, he insists that Word and Sacrament are the sole requisite for the existence of the Church. Opposing the widespread 'spiritual' movement of Anabaptists and others on his left, he insists that without Word and Sacrament there is no Church. In this war on two fronts he seems to be both vindicating evangelical freedom and denying it. In the upshot he comes to emphasize secular authority as having, itself, a special, sacred character; and to lean on it for support. In so far as the medieval world presupposed a clear dualism between the sacred and the secular, Luther is here qualifying it and anticipating the 'secularized Christianity' which it is now fashionable to advocate. He was doing this in his famous doctrine of the *Beruf*, the secular 'Calling' which is itself sacred. He saw that 'secularization' need not be a derogatory term: it may be truly interpreted as the promotion of all things secular, including the State itself, to their place in the divine order.

Luther is not to be identified with later Lutheranism here, nor held responsible for the blatant totalitarianism of *cujus regio, ejus religio* (i.e. the ruler of a State decides on the religion to be professed and practised there). But his dilemma is real; and it does not diminish with the steady penetration of secular authority into the administration of the Church, as local congregations coalesce into large territorial Established Churches. He is unable to escape the old issue of Church and State which was discussed in its ancient imperial context by Augustine (*De Civitate Dei*) and in its medieval feudal context by Dante (*De Monarchia*). He turns to the territorial Princes of Germany in 1520, calling upon them to reform Christendom. He does not doubt their inherent right to do this; nor may we reproach him for being a child of his own time and not a democrat of the twentieth century. Like Calvin he mistrusts the crowd: *man darf dem Pöfel nicht pfeiffen, er tollet sonst gerne* ('the mob goes delightedly wild if you whistle to it'). He assumes—apparently without much misgiving—that in the interest of public order and peace the 'upper classes' should superintend Church Visitations, and suppress teaching which is contrary to the universal faith of Christendom, as clearly founded in Holy Scripture. Ruling Princes should 'crush all faction, uproar and dissension according to the example of Constantine'. The survival of the *ancien régime* in Europe for some three centuries owes more than a little to Luther.

It would seem that he had a reverence for the State as such which is distinctively Teutonic. Both Seeberg and Karl Holl (writing, admittedly, during or just after the First World War) defend him in this and reproach the English-speaking peoples for their lack of this type of patriotism. In one of his great historical essays Holl says of the American, *Er is immer Kolonist geblieben* ('He has always remained a colonist'). Written over fifty years ago, this generalization has probably lost what validity it may once have had; but it is one answer to the easy charge of 'erastianism' which liberal historians have sometimes brought too easily against Luther. There is another answer too. Over against the secular authority of Prince and Magistrate in the Church, legitimizing a necessary minimum of ecclesiastical order, Luther never ceased in his endeavours to secure and preserve the genuine inward freedom of the Church's life.

But the control of the Reformation Church by the Reformation State was not something peculiar to Luther's Germany. Variations apart, this establishment of religion by the State has been the dominant pattern of Protestantism in Scandinavia, Holland, Great Britain and her Dominions. At the local level it has often meant 'the parish muster' rather than a fellowship of believers; it has sometimes meant Squire Western in unholy alliance with the Vicar of Bray.

And yet, the history of the Free Churches in Great Britain reminds us that, without waiting for those rare spirits, John Wesley the Methodist or John Keble the Tractarian, the higher, 'pentecostal' principle persisted along with the workaday compromise. Erastian Protestantism gradually came to tolerate dissent on its left and on its right: it made room, however grudgingly, for the aberrations of Herrnhut, Little Gidding and George Fox. Even the conservative Reformers of the sixteenth century, despite their morbid dread of Ana-baptism, brought with the outward forms for which they were fighting an undiminished sense of faith's indefeasible inwardness.

If the conflicts and divisions of Christendom's classic past are to be replaced in our time by the ecumenical tourney, it will take place within the old and well-defined ecclesiological lists outlined in this chapter. Genuine ecumenism will involve a genuine willingness to learn from history.

SHORT BIBLIOGRAPHY

BURKITT, F. C. *Christian Beginnings*, London, 1924
DODD, C. H. 'Christian Beginnings', *London and Holborn Quart. Rev.*, 1947

CAIRD, G. B. *The Apostolic Age*, Duckworth, 1955
STREETER, B. H. *The Primitive Church*, Macmillan, 1929
HARRISON, P. N. *The Problem of the Pastoral Epistles*, Oxford, 1921
BARTLET, J. V. *Early Church History*, R.T.S., 1925
LIETZMANN, H. *Geschichte der alten Kirche*, Berlin, 1932–38
DUCHESNE, L. *Early History of the Christian Church*, Edinburgh, 1909 (E.T. from 4th French edn.)
—— *Eglises Séparées*, Paris, 1905
—— *Origines du culte chrétien*, Paris, 1920
BAYNES, N. H. *Constantine and the Christian Church*, London, 1916
STEVENSON, J. *A new Eusebius*, Macmillan, 1957
KELLY, J. N. D. *Early Christian Creeds*, Longmans, 1950
SEEBERG, R. *Lehrbuch d. Dogmengeschichte*, I–III, IV. i–IV. ii, 1920–33
LOOFS, F. *Leitfaden z. Stud. der DG*, I–II, Halle, 1906, 4th edn.
HOLL, K. *Augustins innere Entwicklung (Ges. Aufsätze zur KG, III.*, 1928)
GILES, E. *Documents illustrating Papal Authority, A.D. 90–454*, S.P.C.K., 1952
MIRBT, C. *Quellen z. Geschichte des Papsttums und des römischen Katholizismus*, Tübingen, 1924, 4th edn.
FLICHE, A. and MARTIN, V., editors. *Histoire de l'Eglise*, Paris, 1934 f. Vol. VII, 'L'Eglise au pouvoir des laiques' (Amann and Dumas). Vol. VIII, 'La réforme grégorienne (Fliche)
WERNLE, P. *Der evangelische Glaube: I. Luther*, 1918
STROHL, H. 'La notion d'Eglise chez les Réformateurs', *Rev. d'hist. et de phil. rel.*, vol. XVI, 1936
RUPP, G. *Patterns of Reformation*, Epworth, 1970
CONSTANT, G. *La réforme en Angleterre, I.: Le schisme anglican*, Paris, 1930
WHALE, J. S. *The Protestant Tradition*, Cambridge, 1956
PITT, V. *Memorandum of Dissent (Report of the Archbishops' Commission, Church and State*, Eyre and Spottiswoode 1970)

LUTHER'S EUCHARISTIC THEOLOGY
(the main sources, excluding Table Talk and Letters)

1519 A sermon on the blessed Sacrament of the holy and true Body of Christ and on Brotherhood

THE BREACH WITH ROME

1520 A sermon on the new testament, i.e. on the holy Mass

★   Concerning the Babylonish Captivity of the Church

1521 Sermon on the worthy reception of the holy and true Body of Christ

On the abolition of private Masses

On the misuse of the Mass

1522 On receiving the Sacrament in both kinds

THE BREACH WITH THE SPIRITUALS

1523 On reverencing the Sacrament of the holy Body of Christ

★1525 Against the heavenly prophets

1526 Sermon on the Sacrament of the Body and Blood of Christ against the Spirituals (*Schwarmgeister*)

★1527 That these words of Christ 'This is my Body' still stand firm against the Spirituals

★1528 Confession on the Lord's Supper

1529 (The Marburg Colloquy)

★1529 The Greater Catechism

★   The Shorter Catechism

1544 Short Confession on the holy Sacrament

(The foregoing titles are translations from the original German or Latin. Those marked ★ have had great historical importance.)

II

SUPPER AND MASS: THE MEANING
OF CHRISTIAN WORSHIP

A T the tender age of six Thomas Aquinas was taken up to
the battlements at Rossasecca to see the view. He
looked out from the valerian on the walls to the
Abruzzi in the blue distance, and was silent for a long time.
Then he said, 'What is God?' The story is probably apocryphal,
as the best stories often are; yet this one is justified, surely, by
those scholastic systems to which great medieval doctors
devoted their whole lives. Indeed, *Was ist dass Gott heisst?* is the
very question with which Luther's major treatise on the
Eucharist opens: that formidable manifesto of 1527 entitled
'That these words of Christ "This is my Body" still stand'.

Luther himself was a notable product of the later Scholasticism. He, too, is asking here what it means to say 'God'. God
is no 'Object' on which our rational analysis may busy itself,
but ever-acting, omnipresent 'Subject'. He who is far beyond
the outreach of thought is nevertheless nearer to the tiniest
creature than its own ego. He is everywhere and nowhere;
there and not there. He cannot really be found by us in nature
or in history, though these are his works. Such quests end
inevitably in idolatry. How, then, may he be apprehended and
known?

Luther answers that he has willed to be found and known in
his Word. 'That God is there [*da*], and that he is there for thee
[*dir da*], are two different things. He is there for thee when he
adds his Word thereto and says "Here thou must find me" . . .
Though he could be found in stone, fire, water or rope, it is
not his will that I should throw myself into fire or water, or
hang by the rope . . . groping or fumbling for God in any and
every place. For he has ordained a certain way wherein men
are to find him, namely his Word. . . . The whole life and
substance of the Church is in the Word.'

THE WORD

Revived as a theological slogan in the twentieth century, what did 'the Word' mean for Luther in the sixteenth? I suggest a sixfold answer.

It meant, first, the essential content of the Gospel. Luther uses a classic phrase to define this: 'Christ the Son of God is our Saviour': five German words recalling the five Greek words hidden in the early Christian symbol of the Fish: *Christus Gottessohn ist unser Heiland.*

Second, the Word is God's medium of revelation. In more than one famous passage Luther insists that, without the Word, Christ's redeeming work on the Cross would avail nothing. 'Whom would it benefit if God caused Christ to die and rise again, but left the victory hidden and unproclaimed? . . . If I would have forgiveness I must not run to the Cross, for there it is not yet dispensed to me. But I must go to the Sacrament or Evangel, where the Word conveys, pours out, proffers and gives to me the forgiveness won on the Cross.' Attacking the Spirituals in 1525 he says: 'If, in accordance with Karlstadt's notions, I were to meditate on Christ's death with so intense a concentration that I actually sweated blood, that wouldn't avail. It would be like thinking hard (until I died) about some treasure-chest filled with guilders, and buried safely for me in some place, but never brought to light and made over to me. It would be like satisfying hunger with the smell of food.' Luther is saying that God's saving deed in Christ *is* real, in itself; but that the treasure becomes ours only through the revealing Word. And so he adds, 'The Word does it. For even if Christ should be given and crucified for us a thousand times, all were profitless if the Word came not to administer it, and to give it to me, and to say This is for thee.'

For Luther the Word is revelation because it is a word of promise. It enters the heart of the believer with all the power of that divine assurance, 'So shall my Word be that goeth forth out of my mouth; it shall not return unto me void, but shall accomplish that which I please'.

In the third place, the Word conquers time; it makes past

and present contemporaneous. History beyond our reach here becomes history for us; 'formerly' becomes 'now'. An event in the inaccessible past is real presence; the pledge that sin is forgiven is no bare sign of a past event, but Calvary here present; the Body and Blood. That Christ's blood was shed, in fact, under Pontius Pilate is *einmalige Geschichte* (history once upon a time); but its mediation through the Word eliminates time. *So ist keine Zeit da.* This is timeless; it *is* from the foundation of the world.

In the fourth place, the Word cannot be received otherwise than by faith, the believer's personal response to it. Whoever believes *has* what the words of institution promise and convey. We may receive the benefits of his Passion in the Mass by no 'works', no strength of ours, but *sola fide*. Sacraments fulfil their purpose not by being performed but by being believed. No sacrament without faith. Even that faith is not man's work but God's gift: we have nothing that we have not received: all is of God. Faith's response to the Word is itself the quickening action of the Word. 'Word and Faith are correlative.'

Fifth, though faith is inherently personal and individual, its operation is indefeasibly social. Luther's earliest published sermon on the Sacrament (1519) expressly includes Brotherhood in its title. The sermon reminds one of the *Didache* and of Justin Martyr, for it says that in bread and wine, constituted of many grains and many grapes and becoming one substance with us as we eat and drink together, our communion in the Body and Blood is corporate communion. We see why Luther will very soon be writing on the abrogation of private masses (1521). Further, the sermon in 1526 uses his image of the cake: 'the holy sacrament makes us brothers and fellow-heirs of the Lord Christ, *dass aus ihm und uns werde ein Kuchen*'. It also enunciates realized eschatology: here believers are already seated together at the Banquet of the heavenly kingdom.

Lastly, the Word witnesses to the 'absurdity' of Christianity. It is biblical and paradoxical, not Aristotelian and rational. As a divine power working in the deeps of man's being, it transcends sophisticated explanation. 'To the Greeks, foolishness' is St. Paul's testimony, and what is there but a coincidence of opposites, a logical contradiction, in Incarnation or Atonement or Resurrection? That the Eternal becomes the temporal; that the Impassible suffers; that the Immortal dies; that God justifies the ungodly; that our bodily life, annihilated in a grave, is nevertheless consummated beyond history in the bosom of the Father—this biblical Word is, as Tertullian put it, certain because it is impossible. (This paradox is further discussed in Chapter V.) Luther coins a word to express what, philosophically speaking, is nonsense. It is *nihilitudo*—the nothingness of mere rationality when compared with the sheer miracle of God's coming to meet and to redeem man in him who is the Word incarnate.

If we ask the obvious question, why this theology of the Word should have led to an irreparable breach with Rome, the answer, in a word, is the Mass. The Reformation, like all great revolutions, was irresolvably complex, involving political, economic and social issues: but, for the Reformers, its fundamental issue was religious; and this found expression in controversy over that focal point and beating heart of the Church's life, the Sacrament. The theology of the Word could not escape the classic problem inherent in it. It is a dual problem. (i) What, precisely, is the relation of the Sacrifice once offered on the Cross to the offering which is made repeatedly at Christian altars? (ii) What is the relation of the Real Presence there to the elements of bread and wine? These separate yet inseparable issues, so notoriously divisive, enter deeply into Luther's break with Rome on the one hand, and his break with the Spirituals on the other. The first of these two issues must be our main concern in this chapter, though it will involve us inevitably in the second also.

ii

OFFERING AND SACRIFICE: THE DIVISIVE EUCHARISTIC PROBLEM

The New Testament document entitled *To the Hebrews* is addressed to Christians of Jewish origin, people whose new faith had involved a break with the sacred tradition of their fathers. *Hebrews* expounds that break in terms of sacrifice and

38

priesthood. It elaborates a contrast between the old and the new.

Under the old covenant priests were themselves sinful men, and the sacrifices which they offered showed by their very repetition that they were imperfect and ineffectual. But under the new and eternal covenant there is one sinless Priest, and one perfect Sacrifice, the Priest himself being the Sacrifice, which is made once for all. The new covenant abolishes the old because it establishes for ever and in a perfect way those redemptive blessings at which the old could only point.

Thus it is a constant theme of the ancient Church that Christian worship is a sacrifice of praise and thanksgiving. The Lord's Supper, its distinctive act of corporate worship from the beginning, is called *eucharistia*, thanksgiving. And as all real worship involves sacrifice, this thanksgiving involves the sacrificial offering and dedication of ourselves, our souls and bodies, to be a reasonable, holy, and lively sacrifice. The great text is Romans 12: 1.

And yet this is not the sole and exclusive conception of Christian worship to which its history bears witness: there is always something else, in paradoxical juxtaposition. By the middle of the second century the Church is beginning to be richly inconsistent. Presupposing and endorsing *Hebrews*, it claims nevertheless to have an actual altar and sacrifice of its own. The interpretation of the Eucharist by the early Fathers is marked by a baffling ambiguity. It can be at once symbolic and realistic; spiritual yet material. It can come near to putting the new wine back into the old wine-skins. One recalls Harnack's shrewd reflection that the words of institution 'Do this' (*touto poieite*) could be taken so easily to mean 'Sacrifice this' (*touto thueite*) by converts from a heathen context, where *poiein* was a technical term for *thuein*.

As early as A.D. 95 *I Clement* is working out a parallel between the ministers of the Eucharist and the levitical priesthood of the Old Testament. Justin Martyr finds the bread and the cup of the Eucharist in Malachi's prophecy of the pure sacrifice which Gentiles would offer in every place. The conception of sacrifice as propitiatory, wholly unknown to the New Testament, is gradually becoming explicit. In his formal exposition of the rite for catechumens, in the fourth century, Cyril of Jerusalem describes it as both spiritual (*pneumatikē*) and propitiatory (*thusia hilasmou*). The elements are no longer bread and wine. They have been mysteriously changed. There is a real offering of the Body and Blood of Christ himself, slain for our sins.

In the West, this increasing sacrificial emphasis becomes markedly sacerdotal also. Here, that transitional figure of the mid-third century, Cyprian, Bishop of Carthage, begins to anticipate the Western Catholicism of the Middle Ages. Cyprian teaches, of course, that the eucharistic sacrifice is bloodless and spiritual, in contrast to the fleshly sacrifices of the heathen and of the ancient Jews. He insists, nevertheless, in his notable sixty-third letter, that 'the sacrifice which we offer is the Passion of the Lord'. And along with this goes its correlative, a new and explicitly sacerdotal view of the ministry. It is a priesthood analogous to that of the sacrificing priests of the Old Testament; it effects atonement for sin. So high a mystery requires something more concrete than the people's sacrifice of praise: the officiating priest must have 'something to offer' as Gwatkin put it. Representing Christ and acting in his stead, his recital of the consecrating words of institution effects a divine transformation in the bread and wine. Thereafter he has 'something to offer': Cyprian describes it as 'real and full sacrifice, in church, to God the Father'.

To summarize this historical development: the early history of the Lord's Supper or Eucharist is marked by three momentous changes, the roots of which are discoverable as early as the age of the Apostolic Fathers.

(i) As the primitive *Agape* lapses and the Meal develops into a ritual act of worship, a religious fellowship becomes a formal ecclesiastical cultus.

(ii) The Body (*soma*) of Christ with its New Covenant or Testament (*kaine diatheke*) becomes 'flesh and blood'. The old sense of Christ's living presence (*praesentia vivi Christi*) is giving place to something different and new.

(iii) The Supper becomes a Sacrifice, and the door is thereby opening to elements which, strictly speaking, are alien to the witness of the New Testament.

To return to Cyprian, what precisely does his language mean? There is an ambiguity in all eucharistic exposition. It appears in the words which recur unavoidably, such as 'figure', 'sign', 'type', 'likeness', 'representation'. The Latin word *representare* plays a large role in the eucharistic theology of the West, thanks to its ambiguity. Here in the third century we have the historic transition from one of its meanings to another. The word may mean 'representation'; that is, a demonstration, a showing forth. Or it may mean 're-presentation'; that is, a repetition, a re-enactment. Is the Eucharist, then, a representation, a showing forth of Christ's sacrifice: something which God is doing to influence and bless us? Or is it a re-presentation, a repetition and fresh offering of Christ's sacrifice: something which man is doing to influence God and to secure his blessing?

The latter rather than the former emphasis becomes dominant in the Western Church of the Middle Ages. After the moment of consecration the Body and Blood of the immaculate Victim is upon the altar, and is then offered up. The central moment of the whole ritual is the rite of Elevation which follows. The sacramental repetition is thus an actual repetition of that sacrifice once offered on Calvary. It effects propitiation for the sin of the world. The succinct and noble language of the Canon of the Mass, which has long since become part of the very life of Christendom, is its lasting monument.

Liturgical issues are ultimately theological. There is always an intimate link between what Christian men believe about their redemptive relationship with God and the forms of worship which express it. Indeed, the liturgical change which establishes itself as the ancient Church of the Fathers develops into the medieval Church of the Schoolmen, is nothing fortuitous, haphazard or perverse. It is the logical expression of a theological conviction which wins its way in the keen eucharistic debates of the eleventh century and becomes the great dogma of Transubstantiation in the thirteenth.

Over three hundred years ago, John Selden's *Table Talk* could briskly dismiss Transubstantiation as 'rhetoric turned into logic'. Whether this was or was not valid criticism, Professor Burkitt's evaluation is preferable: 'medieval logic uncontrolled by historical criticism'.

But perhaps it is the Swedish theologian, Bishop Gustav Aulén, who has put his persuasive finger on the significant theological issue behind this logic. His sympathies being with the Greek Fathers of the Ancient Church, his studies in the history of doctrine have sought to show that our customary approach to soteriology in the West, Protestant as well as Catholic, has been at least one-sided. Its concern has been with the moral issues of atonement. Its categories, drawn from Temple or Law Court, have been almost exclusively sacrificial or forensic. Aulén seeks to redress the balance, taking seriously the Greek concern with the ontological issues of restoration: the realistic, theurgic categories of re-creation and deification. In short, Aulén argues that the classic patristic witness is to Christ as Victor rather than as Victim: the Eucharist as the conveyance of God's gracious gift to estranged humanity, rather than man's propitiatory satisfaction to estranged divinity. All is of God: that the redeeming initiative is with him is the very meaning of grace. Aulén points to 2 Cor. 5: 19 ('God was in Christ reconciling the world to himself'), and he would endorse those words of Augustine which our own *Dogmatiker*, R. S. Franks, quoted so often: 'there is no greater invitation to love than to be first in loving'.

Aulén may be right, therefore, in making Anselm a turning-point: in tracing to him a change of emphasis in medieval thinking round about A.D. 1100. The *Cur Deus Homo* is really a deviation from the 'classic' line of Christian thought; and this change of direction will influence eucharistic thought and practice. Medieval concern with merit began seriously with Anselm; and this emphasis on the meritorious sacrifice offered by Christ as Man tended, as time went on, to obscure, if not to set aside, its significance as a divine sacrifice, wherein God is in Christ giving himself to the uttermost to reconcile the world to himself. The door is thus opened, says Aulén, towards a conception and use of the Eucharist as 'an instrument of the Church for bringing influence to bear upon God'.

This, of course, is the rationale of private masses and masses for the dead. We noticed in the previous chapter that for Catholic ecclesiology a worshipping community is not vital: mass may be said by a priest with no one present. True, the whole Church on earth and in heaven is ideally present, since the Body of Christ is present: the size of the actual congregation is therefore irrelevant. But as the Middle Ages waned, the gross actuality of private masses became their own condemnation. There were masses for success in business; for fine weather or rain; for the recovery of stolen goods; for the capture of thieves; back in the dark age of the seventh century for compassing the death of a personal enemy. The application of this long-standing practice to the Christian dead, presumed to be in Purgatory, was logical and inevitable. The devout and learned Catholic, Adrian Fortescue, himself explains that, as a propitiatory sacrifice, each mass is a meritorious act in the sight of God: it has a precise value which permits arithmetical calculation: two masses are worth twice as much as one. From such a tariff it was seriously calculated how many were required to bring a soul through Purgatory to Paradise. Quantity being the criterion, priests were employed on a huge scale to say or sing masses at chantry-altars or at the tombs of the wealthy, as a business transaction. In the little university town of Wittenberg in 1510, the Castle church had over sixty clergy to perform some nine thousand commemorative masses annually (Rupp, *op. cit.* p. 51). There is no need to mention the related abuse of the complex system of Indulgences except to say that even a Tetzel was supported by church authority, and made a doctor of divinity. One cites such disorders, some of them nakedly simoniacal, only to illustrate and underline Aulén's theological criticism of the medieval mass (p. 42 above) as an 'instrument for bringing influence to bear upon God'.

iii

THE BREACH WITH ROME

Revolt came like the relentless pressure of flood-water on an inadequate dyke. But the widespread demand for the ending of particular abuses is hardly adequate to explain the tragic break. Despite its own grievous faults and mistakes, the Reformation was an attempt to rebuild on religious fundamentals. By 1520, in his *Babylonish Captivity of the Church*, that reluctant and conservative revel, Martin Luther, found himself laying the axe at the theological root of the tree. Man's inveterate legalism had presumed to erect the very sacrament of redeeming grace into an instrument for doing contractual business with the Holy One, commercializing the benefits of Christ's Passion, and earning salvation. Christ's gift of his atoning sacrifice to believing men had become a meritorious 'good work' in the sacrifice of the Mass. Judged by the scriptural Evangel, this is *Missbrauch* (perversion). It is *eine Tzauberey* (witchcraft). The holy Gospel is *auf dem Kopf gestellt* (turned topsy turvy). 'We come in our pride . . . to give to him, as a work of ours, what we should receive as his gift to us . . . The testator is no longer the bestower but the receiver.'

Calvin makes the same onslaught. His powerful attack on the medieval Mass develops steadily from one section of his *Institutio* in 1536 to a whole chapter of the final edition in 1559. The Roman doctrine is the real enemy in that it not only profanes the Eucharist but annihilates it. Man's presumption would repeat the sacrifice once offered as his own propitiatory sacrifice; and man's legalism would extract merit from God's supreme gift. Man makes God his debtor. For Calvin, as for all the Reformers, this is manifold impiety: it is *horrendae abominationis caput* (*the* frightful abomination).

This theological revolution had inevitable liturgical consequences. First, the correlative concepts of transubstantiation and propitiatory sacrifice are repudiated. In the Lord's Supper the Mass returns to the simplicity of its New Testament model. As Luther put it in his momentous manifesto of 1520, 'the more closely the Mass resembles the first Mass of all which Christ made in the Supper, the more Christian it is'. The Supper thus regains its lost significance as a ritual meal of communion. (How far has subsequent experience authenticated this claim? A searching question.)

Again, the Words of Institution are no longer regarded as a priestly act of consecration effecting a divine miracle. 'The Body and Blood are truly there', says Luther, 'not because of our pronouncement of these words; nor that these words, duly pronounced, may have this efficacy; but because Christ commanded us to speak thus, and to do what he himself did in the first Supper. In this way he united (*conjunxit*) his command and act with our recital thereof.' And Calvin's terse verdict 'we may not imagine any magical incantation here' matches that of the *Formula of Concord* (its *Firm Declaration*, section vii).

Again, Communion in both kinds is restored. The Cup is no longer withheld from the people, though Luther sees this as a relatively indifferent change, since the Word and Faith are the essential reality of the Supper. In 1522 he argues that the restoration of the Cup should be undertaken with proper caution and with care for tender consciences. But by 1520 he had already disputed the right of the Pope to make such changes, adding with grim debating humour 'otherwise he might also refuse the Bread to the people'.

For the vindication of such changes the Reformers appealed to Christ's institution and to the practice of the primitive Church. But a bare summary tends to give too negative an impression. The reforming changes of Luther and Melanchthon, Bucer and Oecolampadius, Calvin and Cranmer were positive rather than negative, conservative and constructive rather than iconoclastic. The gap between Catholicism and Protestantism was and often is less wide in fact than the professional polemic of partisans might suggest. This is the tragedy of the Reformation and the pathos of history.

On the really divisive issue, for example, the Reformers did not make the mistake of rejecting the eucharistic concept of sacrifice. 'The Christian sacrifice', says Luther, 'is prayer and self-offering in God's service, of which all Christians are capable through their priesthood . . .' 'We offer up ourselves together with Christ', he says in another place, 'casting ourselves upon him with sure faith in his covenant. . . .' Again, 'We do not offer Christ but he offers us. He is our *Pfarrer und Pfaff* (parson and pope) in heaven, before the face of God.' The truth is that the Reformers not only returned to the New Testament and to the oldest existing interpretation of 'This is my Body', i.e. that the Church is the Body of Christ, and that feeding upon him its members are organically at one with him and with one another: the Reformers were also returning to the Fathers, and to the thought which is common to Cyprian, Chrysostom and Augustine, that inasmuch as the Church is

Christ's Body, the oblation in the Eucharist is the oblation of the Church itself. Protestants have not forgotten the words of Augustine, 'the offering of the altar shows the Church that she herself is being offered'. As he put it also in one of his letters, 'since you are the Body of Christ and his members, it is *your* mystery that is being placed on the Lord's Table' (Ep. 272).

Should our Protestantism find any serious difficulty, then, in the late Professor Quick's statement: 'the Eucharist is truly a sacrifice, for it is the externalization in human ritual of the self-offering of Christ which was once for all in fact externalized on Calvary'? I think not. It seems sound theology to me, a Protestant Free Churchman, to say that the sacrifice which the divine Redeemer once offered in perfect obedience was a representative sacrifice. The Church, his Body, ever participates therein with thanksgiving. Christ-in-his-Church thus offers the Church-in-himself. And he who makes this offering accepts it, since he who is one with us for ever is also for ever one with the Father. In him God calls saying 'Come unto Me'; and in him Man makes answer saying 'Lo, I am come, to do thy will'. 'Christ our Passover is sacrificed for us', wrote St. Paul, 'let us keep the feast.'

Is there still insuperable difficulty about healing the breach with Rome and keeping the feast of reconciliation? It is the vital question; and (let us be realistic about this) the answer given by history is hardly encouraging to ecumenical idealists.

Forty English men and women, the Catholic martyrs of four hundred years ago, were recently canonized by Rome. 'They died', as Cardinal Heenan rightly put it, 'rather than exchange the sacrifice of the Mass for a Communion service.' Even though his statement simplifies a complex issue, it remains true: just as it remains true that the many Protestant martyrs of four hundred years ago died rather than exchange the Communion service for the sacrifice of the Mass: and just as it remains true that large numbers of quiet people throughout Europe at that time, 'Anabaptists' and 'Spirituals', were the innocent victims of the same savageries (burning at the stake, drowning, disembowelling) at the zealous bidding of Thomas More,

Zwingli, Luther, Calvin and Cranmer. The times were as cruel as our own, and the reconciliation of conflicting 'ideologies' was the insuperable problem that it still is.

It is depressingly instructive to notice that while the break with Rome was recent and still reparable, the moderate Melanchthon foresaw the magnitude of the coming disaster, and advocated conference. A scholar and a theologian, he believed that reconciliation was still possible. Historians still discuss whether he was not, on other grounds, an alien rather than an ally in the Lutheran ranks: here, at any rate, events defeated him. Thanks to the complexity of the total religious, political and social situation throughout Western and Northern Europe, in part the legacy of the waning Middle Ages, the Protestantism which was now emerging was no monolithic structure. The leading Reformers gradually lost their initial unanimity; and despite the ecumenical efforts of men such as Bucer to build a comprehensive liturgical and theological structure in place of the old, national establishments and dissenting forms of Protestant radicalism became the monuments to their failure.

Protestantism's fatal fissiparous tendency disclosed itself before the Marburg Colloquy first dramatized it in 1529. The important corrective research of modern scholars such as Bender, Littell, Williams and Rupp on the Protestantism of the left wing has long established the fact that 'we too easily treat Luther as the norm of the Reformation'. The eucharistic standpoints of the Reformers range from Luther on the extreme right, Calvin on the right, Melanchthon and Bucer at the centre, Oecolampadius and Zwingli on the left, and Spirituals (so called) on the extreme left. The perennial problems of social justice also affected theological debate and judged it. There was more than a streak of conservatism in Luther, the great rebel. He saw rebellion which 'is as witchcraft' in the pathetic revolt of peasants against tyrannous feudal privilege in 1525: it compromised and threatened to ruin the whole precarious enterprise of Reformation. His savagery against the peasants, like that of Augustine against the Donatists, has left a stain on his memory which is indelible.

BREACHES WITHIN PROTESTANTISM

This brings us to divisive eucharistic issues which are still with us. So far we have been concerned with the Reformation as a breach with Rome. We must now consider breaches within Protestantism itself, to which our historic Independency or Congregationalism is one of the monuments.

At war with papal error, Luther and Calvin found themselves compelled to fight error equally unscriptural in the radicalism of the men of their own household: the subjectivism of an *inward* Word which showed itself hostile or superior to the use of almost all outward forms in religion, and virtually threatened to empty Christianity of its objective historical content. Luther's terrible onslaught *Against the heavenly Prophets* (1525) is a monument to the massive conservatism which informed all his reforming activity and which refused to agree that the churchmanship of the Christian centuries might be resolved into the speculative fancies and uncontrollable inspirations of a new gnosticism. The Reformers' answer to such fanaticism (*Schwärmerei*) was twofold.

In the first place, just as the Creator uses the creatures as instruments of his creative activity, so he uses the outward things of sense as means of grace. 'What God does and effects in us, he wills to do through outward means.' 'For the spread of his holy Gospel he deals with us in twofold fashion, outwardly and inwardly. Outwardly he deals with us through the spoken Word of the Gospel and through material signs, viz. Baptism and Sacrament. Inwardly he deals with us through the Holy Spirit and faith, along with other gifts; but in such measure and order that the outward element has to come first, the inward after and through the outward. God has so ordered it that he gives men the inward element only through the outward.' The theologies and formal Confessions of the Lutheran and Reformed traditions are all consistently faithful to this familiar sacramental principle. 'In this way', writes Calvin, 'the merciful Lord here accommodates himself to our capacity. For since we are animal in our nature, ever earth-bound and flesh-bound and neither thinking nor conceiving of aught that is truly spiritual, God leads us to himself through these carnal elements.' This is the thought and the very language of Aquinas.

In the second place the Reformers saw in this spiritualist abuse of the *sola fide* principle a new legalism of faith, even more deadly than that of works against which it was ostensibly directed. True, they had insisted that there is no sacrament without faith (*nullum sacramentum sine fide*); but the indispensability of faith for the fruitful reception of the sacrament means, not that the Christian builds on his faith as such at the Table of the Lord, but on the strengthening succour of the Word actively conveyed to him there. Vital to the sacrament is the objective fact rather than the subjective condition. Calvin speaks for the Lutheran as well as for the Reformed tradition in denouncing as a *présomption diabolique* the contention of certain 'Spirituals' that faith has no need of external means of grace, but that a visible cultus-act might be conceded to those of defective spirituality; 'as if', to quote Calvin's acid comment, 'the Saviour's Feast were an A.B.C. for the illiterate'. For him and for all the Reformers the decisive proof that our weak and vacillating faith needs daily assurance and renewal lies in the only possible answer to an inescapable question: do I confess myself a sinner? 'For if they confess themselves sinners—which, whether they will or not, they must needs do—they must of necessity impute this very quality to the imperfections of their faith.'

In short, though the Eucharist obviously presupposes personal faith, it is essentially the Sacrament of the Word. The tensions resulting from this coinherence of *verbum* and *fides* gave rise to notorious struggles, notably the divisive struggle between Luther and Zwingli. Luther's attacks on the 'Spirituals' usually included not only Karlstadt, Schwenkfeld and others, but also Zwingli. Calvin, too, pronounced what he had read of the Swiss reformer's writings 'profane'. Protestantism at war with itself! Hardly an ecumenical prospect.

It is said that as Karl Barth once left a meeting dominated by some of his intransigeant disciples, he murmured 'Thank God I'm not a Barthian.' Modern research is emphasizing what has long been known, viz. that Zwingli was not a Zwinglian. He was a competent theologian of unchallengeable credal orthodoxy, nor was there anything unworthy about his witness to the strictly spiritual character of faith. This did lead, however, to the negations of his middle period, when he insisted that objects of sense are not ultimately necessary in the realm of the Spirit. They may be symbols, but not indispensable means. Spirit requires no vehicle (*vehiculum Spiritui non est necessarium*). Faith is the sole requisite. Let a man lack faith, and the whole Jordan pouring over him will avail nothing. Zwingli's belief in the Real Presence is indubitable; yet his statement of it throughout is 'subjective'. He speaks, as do all theologians on occasion, of spiritual partaking, allegorical eating (*manducatio allegorica*). *Est* must be translated 'signifies'. 'Eat' in John 6 means 'believe'. To say that the Body of Christ is eaten (*esum*) means that we believingly confess that it was slain (*caesum*) for us. Christ's Body *is* present, therefore, but through the exercise of faith (*contemplatione fidei*) rather than *per essentiam et realiter*. The presence is hardly 'realized' by these anxious disclaimers. In all this entirely intelligible and justifiable caution there is little of that sense, universal in the ancient world, that a sacrament is more than a symbol: that it conveys what it symbolizes and, in some sense, *is* what it symbolizes.

The difference between Zwingli and Luther here is one of accent; between the philsophical mysticism of the Renaissance and the factual 'givenness' of the Word in Reformation theology. It suggests Tillich's distinction between sign and symbol. A sign, he says, bears no necessary relation to that to which it points (a label on a bottle of medicine; a signpost to the next village). But a symbol participates in the reality of that for which it stands (like daffodils in spring; like the ring in marriage; like the flag in patriotism). The sign can be changed arbitrarily, 'whereas the symbol grows or dies according to the correlation between that which is symbolized and those who receive it as a symbol'. As Luther once observed in his *Table Talk*, 'philosophical and theological symbols are not synonymous: a *signum philosophicum* is a symbol of something which is not here (*nota absentis rei*); whereas a *signum theologicum* is *nota praesentis rei*, a symbol of something which *is* here'. In that treatise of 1527 he makes the same point: 'the Eucharist is not a symbol of something absent or future'.

Calvin's criticism of Zwingli is relevant here, namely that his account of faith is deplorably intellectual. It is an act of the understanding rather than a relationship of being. Zwingli may claim that John 6:63 is his 'amulet', his 'irrefragable diamond', the 'iron bastion' of his position—'It is the Spirit that quickeneth; the flesh profiteth nothing. The words that I speak unto you, they are spirit and they are life.' But, says Calvin, he has no awareness of what that sublime discourse means by the bread of life, or by the life-giving flesh of Christ (*caro vivifica Christi*). Calvin is referring, of course, to that text only ten verses away from Zwingli's proof-text: 'Except ye eat the flesh of the Son of Man and drink his blood, ye have no life in you.' Calvin's complaint is that Zwingli discusses faith as though it were merely an act of the understanding or of the imagination whereby a man reminds himself of certain truths; whereas the relationship of faith between Christ and Christians produces and includes that relationship of being, that true partaking of Christ by the soul, which is just what the sacramental language of John 6 is intended to convey.

Yet the Eucharist had a fourfold positive meaning for Zwingli, which Protestantism in general would hardly repudiate as untrue.

First, it is a memorial rite (*commemoratio mortis Christi*) wherein 'you call to mind again that the Body of the Son of God, your Lord and Master, was given for you'. Just as the annual Commemoration Day of the Swiss Confederates recalls the battle of Murten so, by Christ's command, this Meal commemorates his death for man's salvation.

Second, therefore, it is a rite of thanksgiving 'called Eucharist by the Greeks'. 'I have shouted myself hoarse', says Zwingli, 'in showing that "Do this in remembrance of me" must refer to thanksgiving, and not to effecting the presence of Christ's Body (*non ad facturam corporis*).' The Eucharist is *collaudatio* and *cantatio* in grateful memory of what Christ has done for us in his death.

Third, the Eucharist is public testimony of their faith which Christians make to one another and to the world. It is a confessional act whereby the Christian soldier testifies to his membership in the army of Christ. This fellowship-meal of gratitude and thanksgiving is a symbol and a reminder of the soldier's duty to his king. The emphasis is not on a heavenly gift (*Gabe*) but on an earthly duty (*Aufgabe*). Basing his grammatical exegesis of the word '*sacramentum*' on Varro, Zwingli interprets it as public initiation or pledge (*publica consignatio*). Whereas for Luther the Eucharist is Christ's pledge to us, for Zwingli it is little more than our pledge to our Christian neighbours. In one passage he actually writes that the sacraments 'make the whole Church, rather than thee, more certain of thy faith' (*reddunt ecclesiam totam potius certiorem de tua fide quam te*).

Fourth, since the Eucharist is the Sign whereby those who believe give mutual proof thereof, it follows that its ethical and social implications are all-important. Like the covenant oath of the Confederates, periodically renewed, the Eucharist is a common vow of mutual obligation binding believers to one another in Christian love, and involving excommunication as the logical consequence of its dishonour. On this last point there is no disagreement among the Reformers, of course. It is the obvious witness of the New Testament that the sacraments of the Christian religion are indefeasibly social in their implication. Much facile nonsense written about Protestant individualism cannot stand up to serious examination.

Thanks to the decisive break between Luther and Zwingli at Marburg, the contrast between their respective eucharistic standpoints can be overdramatized. Yet the evidence for Luther's realism here is unambiguous and ample. Further, the main issue which divides the Lutheran and Reformed traditions lies here. Fundamentally it is the centuries-old christological problem, and we have to consider it in the following chapter.

To get at Luther's meaning we have first to face what he says. His writings abound in statements such as this: 'the believer eats and receives Christ's Body truly and physically (*wahrhaftig und leiblich*)'. The theme of the treatise of 1523 '*On reverencing the Sacrament of the holy Body*' matches its title: the Body and Blood are really there, and the believer may not refuse them *Anbetung* (reverence). This is but a step away from 'Reservation'. To the end of Luther's life, as his *Short Confession* of 1544 shows, his realism can be crude and intransigeant.

'I lump them all together . . . who will not believe that the Lord's word in the holy Supper is *sein rechter naturlicher Leib* (his real natural Body) received as certainly by Judas or the godless as by St. Peter.' Those whom he thus lumped together were, in their turn, equally unsparing of him. They did not allow him to forget the fatal paragraph in his *Confession* of 1528 which they rightly branded as 'Capernaite'. (The adjective is derived from the Jews of Capernaum who 'strove among themselves saying How can this man give us his flesh to eat?' Iohn 6: 52.) The offensive sentence praised the medieval Pope Nicholas II for compelling Berengar to sign the confession that Christ's Body in the Eucharist is crushed and ground with the teeth: it continued 'would to God that all the Popes had acted in all matters in so Christian a way as did this pope towards Berengar'. In the same treatise one sentence reads, 'it is no great matter whether bread remains or not'; and another, 'it is enough for me that Christ's Blood is there; as for the wine, that is God's affair (*es gehe dem Wein wie Gott will*)'. We must notice in our next chapter that such statements illustrate Luther's virtual indifference to the issue of Transubstantiation and Consubstantiation. Despite the popular view, Luther never used the latter term.

Dangerously extravagant though the expression of Luther's eucharistic realism obviously is, its importance lies in what it means. In the main, its meaning is twofold. First, it witnesses to Luther's dogged religious certainty that in this Sacrament the historic past is really present. 'Christ's Blood is shed when it is dispensed for me and to me.' Such words mean that he has real experience of what once took place; that is, of what is now taking place again. Calvin comes very near to saying the same thing in the seventeenth and eighteenth chapters of Book IV. 'For the covenant which he consecrated once, in his blood, he in a measure renews or rather continues (*quodammodo renovat, vel potius continuat*) for the confirming of our faith.' And in the next chapter he writes: 'nevertheless we do not deny that Christ's immolation is there shown to us (*monstretur illic*)'. It can hardly be denied that Luther and Calvin are here being faithful to the true Catholic tradition. In the second place, Luther's eucharistic realism illustrates his ineluctable sense that the Christian revelation is historical and factual. The Christ who is verily present is not only (if one may put it so) the second person of the Trinity, but the Man of flesh and blood going to his death to achieve the world's redemption. In short, it is the God/Man in his indefeasibly corporeal humanity who is present. Without the Giver there is no Gift.

This is the religion underlying the Lutheran *EST* which said 'No' to the Zwinglian *SIGNIFICAT*, and over the theological expression of which the Reformation movement divided into the two parallel traditions, the Lutheran and the Reformed. We must consider this further in the chapter which follows.

SHORT BIBLIOGRAPHY

FORTESCUE, A. K. *The Mass: a study in the Roman Liturgy*, London, 1922

RAUSCHEN, G. *Monumenta eucharistica et liturgica vetustissima*, Bonn, 1914. (*Florilegium Patristicum*, Fasc. vii)

HEADLAM, A. C. and DUNKERLEY, R. (editors). *The Ministry and the Sacraments*, S.C.M., 1937

STONE, D. *A History of the Doctrine of the Holy Eucharist*, Oxford, 1909

AULÉN, G. E. H. *Christus Victor*, S.P.C.K., 1931

—— *The Swedish Lutheran Church* (in 'Headlam and Dunkerley' cited above)

—— *Reformation and Catholicity*, Edinburgh, 1960

—— *The Faith of the Christian Church*, S.C.M., 1961

MOZLEY, J. K. *The Doctrine of the Atonement*, Duckworth, 1927

HOLL, K. *Luther* (*Gesammelte Aufsätze*, I, 1923)

FRANKS, R. S. *A History of the Doctrine of the Work of Christ*, 2 vols., Hodder, 1918

—— *The Doctrine of the Trinity*, Duckworth, 1953

WILES, M. *Some Reflections on the Origins of the Doctrine of the Trinity*, J.T.S., April 1957

WERNLE, P. *Der evangelische Glaube*, II Zwingli, 1919

ZWINGLI. *De vera et falsa religione commentarius*, 1525

ZWINGLI. *Subsidium de Eucharistia*, 1525

—— *Amica exegesis, i.e. Expositio Eucharistiae negotii*, 1527
(Werke: ed. Egli, Finsler und Köhler, 1905 f.)

ACTON, LORD. *Lectures on Modern History*, Macmillan, 1921

LOOFS, F. Art. '*Abendmahl*', II (in *Realencycl.*, 3rd edn.)

DALE, R. W. *The Epistle to the Ephesians*, Hodder, 1882

—— *Essays and Addresses*, Hodder, 1899

RUPP, G. *op. cit.* p. 33 above

III

SIGN AND REALITY: THE MODE OF THE
REAL PRESENCE

WHEN *The Person and Place of Christ* by P. T. Forsyth was published some sixty years ago, my father-in-law, H. C. Carter, ordered a copy. The book duly arrived, invoiced as *The person in place of Christ*. Forsyth would have appreciated the irony. Had he not himself deplored the replacement of the positive preaching of the past by the modern mind? He was no tiresome reactionary, of course. He knew that old problems yield place to new, and that in actual fact men never merely endorse the orthodoxies of their fathers. But Forsyth did take our fathers of the reformed tradition seriously, even though their works were now only sixpence a volume octavo along the pavements of the Charing Cross Road. He learned even from their astonishing controversies which are now so dated. In this chapter, I propose to try to do just that; for the eucharistic controversy which has divided Protestantism for over four centuries still has its relevance. It is still no trivial obstacle to reunion.

Controversy. Not about the undisputed fact of the 'real presence' but about its mode: what Bonhöffer described as the fatal *'wie' Frage*, the 'how' question. Writing in 1525 to Bugenhagen in Wittenberg, Schwenkfeld demanded, 'What, then, do you actually eat in the Supper; the mortal or the glorified Body? Is Christ there corporally or spiritually?' For Zwingli, too, this was the obvious issue. His ally Oecolampadius in Basle reviewed the Lutheran *Syngramma* with the complaint 'you devote almost a quarter of your book to saying that the bread has the Word but not even a syllable to demonstrating how'. The issue was tersely summarized by Calvin: *de modo quaestio est* (the question is how).

All Luther's writings register his dislike of rationalizing speculation here. After 1520 he mildly rejected Transubstantiation, but he regarded it as an error of no great import (*an diesem Irrtum nicht gross gelegen ist*). He himself preferred a similar medieval theory going back to Duns Scotus, namely that the substance of the Body and Blood is present along with that of the bread and wine. He sometimes uses red-hot iron as an illustration of this consubstantiality: two substances—fire and iron—conjoined in unity. But the famous term Consubstantiation is not found anywhere in his writings, despite its not infrequent use in contemporary controversy. Luther suspects and fears all such *Subtiligkeit* (cleverness). Later in this chapter we must pay proper respect, of course, to the philosophy of 'substance' presupposed by such a technical term as Transubstantiation.

But what, in fact, was Luther's answer to the fatal 'how' question? I suggest that the key to his notorious intransigeance here is his attitude to two enduring issues of historical theology: the problem of Revelation and the problem of Christology.

i

REVELATION AND REASON

First, Revelation; which has always involved its relation to Reason. It seems to me that Luther's greater treatises on the Eucharist are inherently polemical just because they are monuments to what is almost a formal irrationalism: that 'absurdity' of the Word to which reference was made in the previous chapter. Whereas Zwingli's biblical theology had been influenced by the older scholastic tradition of Aquinas, Luther's had been shaped in the newer scholastic mould of Scotus and William of Ockham, for whom the validity of Christian revelation ultimately rests not on rational considerations but on the sheer contingency of God's sovereign will. Scripture, interpreted by experience, confirmed that irrationalism.

Luther's works contain truculent attacks on Reason as 'the Strumpet', 'the Fool', 'the Devil's Bride': also innumerable statements such as these which are collected together here from separate contexts. 'Even though a hundred thousand devils were to come asking how bread and wine can be the Body and Blood of Christ, I know that all the spirits and learned men together are not as wise as the little finger of the Almighty . . . The Holy Ghost is greater than Aristotle . . . See that thou attend only to the Word and rest therein as a babe in the cradle . . . Here is the stark, clear, simple command on which we rely, "Take, eat, this is my Body" . . . Beware of pin-point speculations like those of Averroës . . . The Holy Spirit is not sceptical . . . Let reason rest . . . God is such a one as to do what, to the world, is foolish and unfitting . . . With regard to the Eucharist we must deny eyes, mouth, and all our senses rather than presume to measure God's will and action with our reason. To ask *how* the Body and Blood is here is to try to imprison God in our own darkness . . . God has ordained that Christ's Body is in the Supper and God's power makes it so.' At Marburg, facing his opponents across the table on which he had chalked the words 'This is my Body', he exclaimed, 'If God ordered me to eat dung I would do it . . . A servant doesn't question his master's will'; thereupon Zwingli protested, understandably, against a biblicism which would use the truth of divine omnipotence to buttress what is really a technical absurdity. Zwingli is certainly not arguing that miracle, as such, is absurd. As he wrote in his *Subsidium* of 1525, 'No believer has ever doubted the Virgin Birth; but none of us really believes that the sacramental bread *is* Christ's flesh . . . This recourse to the marvellous makes God a liar since, in the end, it makes all essential characteristics of the Creation unreliable. Bread can as well be both bread and Christ's Body as man can be at once man and the flower of the field'.

Incidentally, the same issue reappears some twenty years later in Calvin's controversy with his able Lutheran opponents, Westphal and Hesshus. He complains that they stand pat on the word 'is', whereas reverence for scripture compels him to investigate what the sacred text is really saying. He has sympathy with the Lutheran position since it is, fundamentally, his own: like Luther, he regards the Eucharist as a mystery transcending the speculations of reason: but that is why he regards the appeal to omnipotent divine will as the misuse of a legitimate concept. 'For the question is not what God could have done, but what he was in fact pleased to do.'

The issue lies deeper than that of the verbal inerrancy of

scripture. Luther is not guilty of a slavish literalism. The exegetical battle is really a theological battle over the sheer 'givenness' of Revelation through the Word. Luther may say that the text stands like a rock and that every schoolboy of seven knows what the words mean; but he is virtually saying, in the name of a religious metaphysic of sheer absolutism, that the Eucharist is miracle; the supreme miracle of divine grace. In his formidable manifesto of 1527 he actually argues that the bodily 'real presence' is necessary 'for the annihilation of human reason'. This is *nihilitudo* indeed, not to say naughtiness.

If, for Zwingli, the content of the Word is a system of truth which is in some sense rational, for Luther it is not. The content of the Word is the tremendous paradox 'God in the flesh'. The eternal God, who is beyond all conceiving, became truly and fully incarnate in Jesus Christ. Our creaturely finitude was there made *capax infiniti* (capable of the Infinite). But this is not rationally intelligible. Indeed, it means that God is hidden there as well as revealed. The Cross both manifests and hides him. This cannot be rationalized, however much our pride urges us to make the attempt. To quote a profound sentence from the *Table Talk*, 'The world dislikes and can't endure a *deus corporeus* who is born, preaches, convicts the world, is crucified, dies: on the other hand the world strains every nerve to have and worship him as *incorporeus*: thus, however, it can never know him.' This recalls Marshall McLuhan's recent remark, 'Thingness is a scandal to the conceptualist.' It illustrates his antithesis of 'percept' and 'concept': religion dies when the former is made to yield to the latter; that is, when theology takes over from revelation. Here McLuhan is in line with Kierkegaard and Luther.

In short, it is a religious conviction rather than a deliberate flight from reason which explains Luther's stand on the divine omnipotence. But it is ironical that, despite his mistrust of reason here, the Zwinglian charge of *absurditas* stung him into making use of it, with results which only intensified the essential difficulty. Though deeply reluctant, Luther will allow himself to be drawn from his real stronghold in religious experience to the highly speculative field of christological argument, and to indecisive logomachies over the divine ubiquity, the 'right hand of God' and the Ascension. And so we come to the second enduring issue of historical theology: the mystery of Christ's person.

ii

THE TWO-NATURES CHRISTOLOGY

Luther's knowledge of God is wholly christocentric. Strictly speaking, for him God is real only in Jesus Christ. He knows no God save him whom this Man 'embodies'. Luther would have endorsed Ritschl's remark 'without Christ I should be an atheist'. Indeed, he would have warmed to a letter written just fifty years ago by Bernard Manning to his minister and intimate friend, H. C. Carter. It was written from Jesus College, Cambridge, on a Monday morning in the Michaelmas Term after one of those Sundays memorable for worship at Emmanuel and for talk in the evening at Lyndewode Road. It has not been made public until now.

> My dear Henry,
>   It is too bad to inflict still more upon you, but I have just discovered why you feel that I think more of the form and letter, and less of the spirit, than I ought. It all depends really on my belief in the Incarnation. In the incarnate Word I value (if I may put it so without being profane) the Revealer more than the Revealed. The Son is dearer to me than the Father. I love the flesh of Palestine infinitely more than the very God who inhabited it: than the Spirit Whom the flesh was made to make real to us. The Flesh, the Body, the Man, Jesus our Saviour is the whole of my faith, and I cannot care for what he reveals. I want no more. This bias, if I am not mistaken, affects all my love of the medium which reveals. I do not want to see the Father if I may still see the Son; nor the Word if I may love the Flesh. I don't defend what I feel: but quite honestly and simply that is my religion.
>
> Ever yours affectionately,
> Bernard

God forbid that I should label such a document, pigeon-holing it as Lutheran rather than Calvinist. But it is an illuminating commentary on what Luther was defending in the formative

60

days of our Protestantism. It takes us to the heart of christology. Here we must look briefly at the history of doctrine.

Christology is the thought of the Church about the ineffable mystery of Christ's person. After the internecine struggles of the fourth and fifth centuries, that thought is authoritatively defined at Chalcedon: not in the Hebraic idiom of scripture, unfortunately, but in the philosophical thought-forms of the Greek, Byzantine world. Technical terms such as 'essence', 'nature', 'hypostasis', 'person' are hardly typical of the Bible.

The Definition pronounces that Jesus Christ, perfect in godhead and perfect in manhood, is *One Person in two Natures*. Each nature is complete: each is distinct from the other: yet their unity as one person is real and absolute. Chalcedon doesn't say *how* the unity of Christ's person can be a fact, along with the completeness and distinction of the two natures. It ignores the obvious logical and psychological difficulties. This, indeed, is its value and its strength. Modern thought criticizes it drastically on several grounds; yet criticism is largely irrelevant since the historical achievement of Chalcedon has been to leave the paradox as such, and to serve as the authoritative norm, whereby two main views or tendencies—to the right and left of it respectively—are repudiated as abnormal, not to say heretical.

There is the view associated with Antioch, seeking to do justice to the divine Man of the synoptic gospels, but at the risk of jettisoning the unity of his person. Here the two Natures of the Incarnate Christ look dangerously like two Persons. This duo-physite view, explicit in Nestorianism, was condemned at Chalcedon.

On the other hand, there is the view associated with Alexandria—Johannine and transcendental—interpreting Christ as the eternal God incarnate, but at the risk of jettisoning the human Jesus of history. Here the one Person of the incarnate Christ looks dangerously like one Nature. This monophysite view, explicit in Eutychianism, was condemned at Chalcedon.

The claim of Chalcedonian orthodoxy to be the authoritative norm has not always and everywhere been honoured: the Nestorian and Monophysite schisms are monuments to dissent from it. But Chalcedon did fix the exact metaphysical guidelines which have ever since determined the orthodox christology of Christendom—not only Eastern but Western; not only Catholic but Protestant.

The Reformers were not heretics. They were at one with Christendom in confessing the creeds of the ancient Church. Luther and Zwingli presupposed Chalcedon without question. But the difference between them is the difference of accent between Alexandria and Antioch. Admittedly, Luther was no more a Eutychian than was Cyril; and Zwingli was no more a Nestorian than was Theodoret: but whereas Luther looks steadily in a monophysite direction, distinguishing ideally between the two Natures yet insisting on their inseparable cohesion, Zwingli looks steadily the other way; and while not ceasing to hold to the unity of the Person, builds all his thought on the distinction between the two Natures.

As controversy becomes conflict the protagonist is also the antagonist. The eucharistic controversy puts each man on his guard: Luther against a merely nominal union, Zwingli against a merely nominal distinction, between the two famous Natures.

Luther begins and ends with the indissoluble unity of the Person of the God/Man. The two Natures being absolutely inseparable, 'where the one is there the other must be . . . it is the self-same Person who rules the world and is mishandled by devil and man'. Luther uses a classic patristic formula to express and defend this: *communicatio idiomatum*. Translated literally and unhelpfully this means 'the communication of the idioms'. But the word 'idiom' here means a 'characteristic' or 'attribute' of something; and applied to the two Natures of Christ's Person the classic formula means a mutual interchange or reciprocal communication, whereby the human characteristics may rightly be attributed to Christ as God, and the divine characteristics to him as Man (*ut ea quae hominis recte de deo et, e contra, quae dei sunt de homine dicantur*). Godhead and manhood being one Person in Christ the incarnate Word, scripture is alleged to ascribe to his godhead all that pertains to his manhood, and vice versa.

There are obvious and notorious difficulties here, not only for Luther but also for the Fathers to whom he appeals.

Scripture does not dot the i's and cross the t's of patristic speculation so precisely; nor do the Fathers themselves support
Luther's scholasticism here as fully as he implies. He interprets
their formula in three distinct ways which have become
standard doctrine for Lutheranism: only two of them, however,
can be said to have the support of patristic tradition as a whole.

The first way (*idiomaticum*) sees the distinctive characteristics
of each Nature as belonging to the whole Person, which may
therefore be described now in terms of the one and now in
terms of the other. (This 'solves' the insoluble 'complex of
opposites' by restating it in different words, but leaving it
unsolved.)

The second way (*apotelesmaticum*, i.e. productive of a result)
sees each Nature integrally one with the other: the result of
their oneness is the common action which they accomplish.
(This, again, is mere re-assertion of the mystery; it explains the
square root of minus one as 'the square root of minus one'.)

The third way (*majestaticum*) outdoes even the patristic tradition by going beyond it and being explicitly incredible. A
scholastic argument derived from William of Ockham, it
asserts a full communication of the divine characteristics to the
human Nature—not only omnipotence and omniscience but
also omnipresence. (It is the divine characteristic of omnipresence or 'ubiquity' which plays so large a role in Luther's
eucharistic controversy with Zwingli, and re-enforces the
Zwinglian charge of '*absurditas*'.) In short, Luther is here using a
patristic formula to make the stupendous affirmation, not only
that Jesus was omnipresent, but also that God died, 'which',
says Luther, 'is not more wonderful than that he became Man'.
In the Confession of 1528 he writes, 'If I believed that the
human nature alone had suffered and died for me, Christ
would be a wretched Saviour (*ein schlechter Heiland*) who would
himself stand in need of a Saviour.' Further, though Luther
defends himself with energy against the charge of confusing
and mingling the two Natures, what he writes in the manifesto
of 1527 and elsewhere about Christ's actual body of flesh
presses hard in the direction of Eutychianism, the heresy
condemned at Chalcedon. Though visible and palpable,
Christ's body is at the same time flesh permeated with divinity;

'ein Gottesfleisch'; *'ein Geistfleisch'*: it is flesh *'durchgöttert und durchgeistet'*.

What are we to make of this? Does it suffice to say that for four hundred years our tradition as Independents or Congregationalists has been Reformed rather than Lutheran; and that the Reformed christology, broadly speaking, seems to us to recall the historic evidence of the New Testament more faithfully and convincingly here than does the Lutheran? We are not only with Calvin who, as we shall be noticing shortly, could not accept Luther's distinctive interpretation of the *communicatio idiomatum*: if we are to take the Two Natures christology seriously at all today must we not agree also with Zwingli that the interchange of attributes is rhetorical and figurative rather than actual, in those scriptural texts and phrases on which Lutherans have relied here?

iii

MONOPHYSITISM AND SOTERIOLOGY

But even so, there is something else to be said. To understand Luther here we have to see him against the whole christological tradition of Christendom in all its variety and richness: its Eastern and Greek as well as its Scholastic and Western form; and not only the definitive doctrine but also its persisting distortions. We must take a further look at the history of doctrine (and of heresy!), gratefully acknowledging our indebtedness to the learning of H. J. Schoeps in his monograph *Vom himmlischen Fleisch Christi.*

In most periods of church history there have been denials of Christ's *divinity*, from Ebionites in the first century and Arians in the fourth down to Socinians, Unitarians and the extreme Liberals of the modern period.

Rarer, but religiously much more significant, have been the denials of Christ's *humanity*. Various forms of docetism, some of them covert rather than open, have been commoner than one might have supposed: i.e. the view that the flesh which the Redeemer took was different from ours; it was heavenly rather than earthly; his body merely appeared to be flesh and blood.

64

Warnings against this explicit gnosticism are already found in the Fourth Gospel, but it persists and grows. For the Valentinians, a century later, Christ was born, not *of* but *through* the Virgin, 'as through a tube'. His body could know nothing of normal physiological processes such as digestion. In the heresy of Apollinaris (fourth century), not only does the Divine Logos take the place of Christ's human mind; his flesh, too, is divinized and itself has redeeming power. Apollinaris is the real father of the monophysitism, implicit in much Greek Orthodoxy, which Eutyches blurted out explicitly at Chalcedon. Cyril of Alexandria showed more finesse, but Nestorius rightly accused him of marked Apollinarian leanings; the first, but by no means the last, to do so. Cyril's mariology marked a new stage in the developing dogma of the Immaculate Conception: it anticipated Julian of Halicarnassus in the early sixth century, who taught the incorruptibility of the Redeemer's body, since the flesh which he took from the 'Mother of God' could not have been the sinful flesh of a daughter of Adam: it was no more than 'the *likeness* of sinful flesh' (Romans 8: 3). There is a covert monophysitism even in that Aquinas of the Orthodox Greek East, John of Damascus.

But it asserts itself, too, in the Latin West and is notorious in Hilary of Poitiers in the fourth century. For him Christ's body is 'celestial', untouchable by human pain or passion: divinely self-sufficient, and therefore patient of no human needs such as sleep, food or drink. Only by his voluntary decision was his body disrobed of its distinctive impassibility, so that it might receive the onslaught of the evil Powers, to redeeming issues. But even so, he could not really be touched with the feeling of our infirmities: his Passion was suffering, objectively considered, but it was not personal grief (*passus est; non doluit*). Further, his walking on the sea and his transfiguration on Mount Tabor were not so much 'marvels' as characteristic and proper manifestations of his 'heavenly' body.

It is hardly surprising, then, that a gnostic tendency, so deep-seated and widespread, should have reappeared in the Protestantism of the West. Schwenkfeld's theology, strongly influenced by his Greek patristic studies, is at least implicitly monophysite. Melchior Hofmann, leader of the Anabaptists in that city of refuge, Strasburg—like Menno Simons, founder of the important sect of the Mennonites—repeats the teaching of Valentinus that Christ was not born of (*natus ex*) but made in (*factus in*) the body of Mary. A divine Saviour, incarnate in the sinful flesh of Adam, would have been *no* Saviour; his sacrificial offering on the Cross would have been unclean and unavailing.

In Servetus, Paracelsus and lesser known but representative figures such as Valentin Weigel, Nicholas Teting and Paul Felgenhauer, the modern researches of Schoeps and others are making us more than ever aware that this centuries-old desire to divinize the Lord's humanity out of motives of reverence, this unwillingness to accept a truly carnal Incarnation and a fully human Redeemer, was not lacking even in the Protestant West.

It will be rightly objected, of course, that all this is nevertheless pathetic heresy which shatters itself on the testimony of the Synoptics and of the Epistle to the Hebrews: that it is christological phantasy which is not typical of the Catholic or of the Protestant West, but very exceptional. This objection is doubtless sound. Yet such heresy has something to say to us nevertheless: for those who have ears to hear it can disclose important soteriological meaning.

The soteriology which has long since won complete supremacy in the West—in Catholicism and Protestantism; in Mass and Methodist Hymnbook—sees the Redeemer as the divine Man who offers atoning sacrifice to God, qualified thereto by his divine Nature.

The Greek East presents the same mystery differently. It sees the Redeemer as God incarnate rather than as divine Man. The Word becomes Man in order to deify and redeem our mortal and corrupt humanity. We must elaborate this a little.

In the West, whether it be declared in the Mass or in 'Rock of Ages', salvation involves atonement: it is understood in terms of moral and forensic realities: its characteristic language is seen in words such as 'sin', 'guilt', 'penalty', 'grace', 'satisfaction', 'expiation', 'acquittal'. Its imagery is drawn from the law-court, the altar of sacrifice; even the counting-house. The

66

Saviour vindicates the righteousness of God; he is the atoning Victim; he 'pays the mighty debt I owe'.

In the Greek East, salvation is conceived and expressed as a divine therapy inherent in, and communicated through the Incarnation itself. It is the inoculation (so to speak) of corruption with incorruption; of disease with healing. The life of humanity is recapitulated and transformed in and through the life, from cradle to grave, of the true Man, the Man from Heaven, the incarnate Redeemer. Salvation is a process of renewal and restitution, often dramatized as victory over the demonic Powers of corruption and death. Its imagery is drawn not only from the hospital and the laboratory, but from the battlefield. Christ is Victor.

Thus Greek soteriology has a twofold motive and meaning. It could be labelled both 'Antiochene' and 'Alexandrian'. On the one hand, like the Epistle to the Hebrews, it confesses that the incarnate Word must be genuinely incarnate; unambiguously human; like us in all respects—our sin excepted. It says No to its memorable heretic Apollinaris, in the words of its Cappadocian Father, Gregory Nazianzus: 'that which is not assumed is not healed'. If the healing Inoculation is to be effective, the precious Lymph—the Manhood of the Redeemer—must not be impaired or diluted: it must be full and complete: its completeness must not be feigned in any way. Genuine 'recapitulation' means 'being tempted in *all* points like as we are'. But, on the other hand, Greek soteriology insists that the incarnate Redeemer must also be divinely *un*like us: only God can redeem us from the thraldom of decay, and make us 'divine'. It says Yes to the truth which is concealed in its own dangerous, monophysite tradition: it endorses the very words of Apollinaris himself: 'the death of a *man* does not annul Death'.

It is usual to criticize Greek Orthodoxy here on two main grounds. First, the Chalcedonian categories—'two Natures in one Person'—are dismissed as psychologically absurd. But if the 'Word made Flesh' is at all meaningful and true, it involves inescapable paradox; and Chalcedon at least states and preserves what it is beyond the powers of our logic to resolve. Again, we accuse Greek Orthodoxy of having a defective evangelical sense. We quote the verdict of the great Anselm: 'Thou hast not yet considered how great is the weight of sin'. Taught by Dale, Denney and Forsyth we feel that we have not been altogether wrong. Taught by Franks and Tillich we have been alerted to Greek Orthodoxy's in-built inclination 'to read the words of the Synoptic Jesus Christ as if they were the words of the Johannine Christ Jesus'. We rightly fear the potential docetism of Byzantium: it has too often become actual.

These criticisms have their validity. They are useful warnings. But if I say with Paul 'God was in Christ', really meaning what I say, I find that I have a renewed understanding of the serene religious conviction of Greek Orthodoxy that redemption is real only if he who suffers and dies is Victor in the strife, and is divine. The deification of Christ's humanity has always been a strong, albeit dangerous, tendency in Eastern Christendom, just because his unlikeness to us in all respects is as integral to the christological paradox as his likeness to us in all respects. I am not defending this. I am trying to understand it, and the strength of its appeal.

iv

LUTHER'S EUCHARISTIC REALISM

This seems to be the clue to the distinctive elements in Luther's eucharistic theology. He is Eastern as well as Western. For him as for Augustine—that notable bridge between Christian Europe's East and West—Christ is both Victor and Victim. If Calvin is the last and greatest of the Schoolmen (as Streeter put it), Luther is the last and greatest of the 'graecizing Westerns' of the medieval world. This goes far to explain why he stuck so doggedly to so difficult a concept as that of Christ's bodily ubiquity; and why the Lutheran and Reformed traditions have looked askance at one another for so long, declining full reconciliation.

In our Reformed or Calvinist tradition, the Incarnation is a *kenosis*, a divine self-emptying, whereby the Eternal Son submitted, genuinely and completely, to the limitations of man's creaturely life. In the Lutheran tradition, the Incarnation is the exaltation of human nature, in the person of the Logos,

68

into the conditions of the divine life. In short, Lutheran christology emphasizes the majesty of Christ's humanity; Reformed christology insists on its reality.

To come to particulars: Zwingli believed that in the days of his flesh Christ suffered only in his finite human nature. That nature, now in heaven, is finite and limited to a heavenly 'place'. The Body and Blood are not really present, therefore, at the Lord's Table. Only according to his divine nature was and is he omnipresent. Here Luther breaks with him. This divides Christ, and robs his redeeming work of its divine meaning and power. 'What Christian heart can bear this destruction of the whole faith? Wherever Christ is, there is God also . . . Christ is one person, and he does not separate his humanity from himself as Master Hans takes off his coat and lays it by him on going to bed.' Luther always insisted that the 'how' of the Real Presence should be left as ineffable mystery; but he was provoked by continuing opposition to make more than one attempt at a theological rationale.

He has to make 'ubiquity' credible. His method in 1527 is to expound the meaning of the 'Right Hand of God'. Unlike Calvin, he breaks with the conception current since Augustine that Christ's Body is in heaven, i.e. in a particular place (*sonderlicher Ort*) 'like a bird on a tree-top'. The right hand of God is necessarily illocal, since God is omnipresent. It follows that he is entirely, personally present in Christ, 'on earth, in the womb, yea in cradle, temple, desert . . . on the cross, in the grave; yet at the same time in heaven, in the bosom of the Father'.

Since Christ's Body shared and shares in this omnipresence, Luther does not shrink from a threefold consequence: (i) Even the earthly body—admitted to be of spatial magnitude—was omnipresent. (ii) His Body at the illocal right hand of God is nevertheless '*ein ausserlich leiblich Ding* [a thing of outward bodily form] having flesh and bone as he himself says in Luke 24: 39'. (iii) As omnipresent, he is present at every common meal. This last sounds like a sixteenth-century version of the famous Oxyrynchus logion 'Cleave the wood and there thou shalt find me; raise the stone and there am I'. But if it were so, wouldn't it prove too much? Luther would say No, since he distinguishes between Christ's presence and our apprehension thereof. The absolute omnipresence becomes the Real Presence at the Holy Table because Christ has so willed it. His presence is hidden (*abscondita*), apart from the Word, received in the heart by faith.

Luther makes a second attempt in 1528. Here his method is Occamist, closely resembling that of Fisher, Bishop of Rochester, against Oecolampadius the year before. (Church history is not without its ecumenical ironies.) He argues that there are three ways of being 'at a place'. (i) The first—spatial or *circumscriptive*—is like the presence of wine in a cask. This is dismissed at once: the divine presence cannot be expressed in an analogue so coarse and gross. (ii) The second—labelled *diffinitive*—transcends the spatial but is inexplicably related to it: the gospels are evidence that angels or demons may be present in a great or a little space, a city or a house, a demoniac or a herd of swine. Christ's resurrection-body, which knows no spatial limitation, appears spatially as and where he wills. In this mode of 'multivolipresence' he can be, and is, present in the Eucharist. (iii) The third mode—labelled *repletive*—is that of ubiquity proper: the divine omnipresence, incomprehensible to our human understanding.

Apart from the difficulty that the second and third modes are, strictly speaking, mutually exclusive, there is the difficulty of knowing how seriously Luther held to these scholastic arguments. Some authorities discuss whether he had not abandoned the category of ubiquity even while continuing to argue in its defence. They ask where the *prius* of his whole contention lies: with his eucharistic faith, or with his christological doctrine? Would he have elaborated this category of ubiquity at all if the controversy over the mode of the Real Presence had never arisen in 1525? What is certain is that in his last treatise on the Eucharist in 1544 he quotes with warm approval the eighth verse of the Sequence *Lauda Sion Salvatorem*, and adds: 'So the Papists teach; yes, and not only the Papists but the holy Christian Church and we along with it, that Christ's Body is assuredly there, not *localiter* but *diffinitive*; bodily and truly'.

So much, then, for Luther's two scholastic attempts at a rationale. But the question 'how' still presses. 'This is my

Body.' How are these words to be interpreted and understood?

The problem for eucharistic theology of all confessions is the seemingly contemporaneous presence of two 'substances'. The great Roman dogma denies that they *are* contemporaneous: the substance of the bread and wine is transubstantiated into the substance of the Body and Blood, the 'accidents' alone remaining. This metaphysical concept—of 'accidents' subsisting *per se* without a subject—is very difficult to comprehend or even to imagine, of course. Experts in scholastic philosophy are struggling with re-interpretations of it today. Like the elaborate symbolism of nuclear physics—where the atom dissolves into a kind of solar system, and matter into mystery—it is a huge hypothetical construction to account for what is impenetrable to the coarse finger of investigation. No one has seen or ever will see an electron. And 'substance' which is transubstantiated, its accidents alone remaining, is (like the Cheshire Cat which vanished leaving only its smile) a metaphysical alchemy which is necessarily inscrutable.

Zwingli's doctrine is like the Roman in that it, too, makes the same denial. The two 'substances' are not contemporaneous. But holding firmly to the substance of the bread and wine, he gives up the substantial presence of the Body and Blood.

Luther's doctrine is consonant with his christology. There *is* a sacramental union of two distinguishable substances, 'despite the pin-pricking sophistry of logicians'. This is not essential unity, like that of the Father and the Son; nor personal unity, like that of Christ's two natures; nor formal unity like that between the Spirit and the form of a dove; nor a unity of mingling, as though the bread made with the Body a *tertium quid*.

Luther appeals (and here there is yet another attempt at a rationale) to that figure of speech whereby one names a complex whole, such as a purse, but means only a part of it—the hundred guilders which it contains. He dismisses the obvious difficulty that purse and guilders form no real unity; he says that they do (*die zwei Wesen sind in ein Wesen gekommen*). So, too, the bread of the Eucharist is no longer bakehouse bread but *Leibsbrot*: it is bread which, with the Body of Christ, is *ein*

71

sakramentlich Wesen und ein Ding (one sacramental entity and one thing).

This has far-reaching implications. It involves *manducatio oralis* (eating with the mouth); the physical partaking of the Body and Blood. And Luther did honestly and very rashly endorse the revolting words of the Confession extorted from Berengar in 1059. Again, it involves *manducatio indignorum* (partaking by the unworthy) who must include, on Luther's presuppositions, not only unbelievers, but animals. There was debate, as inevitable as it was deplorable, about the fragment of the bread which might be dropped and consumed by the church mouse. The Lutheran Brenz not only insisted that unbelievers eat the Body and Blood (to their deadly hurt, as in 1 Cor. 11: 29), but that mouse or rat may do so, 'otherwise the power of the mouse is necessarily stronger than the word of our Lord Jesus Christ'. We should remember, in passing, that Luther was not wrong in principle here. *All* who partake of this sacrament are unworthy to do so: 'there is none righteous, no not one'. The Gospel of God's grace which is declared and realized at the Holy Table is for sinners. Being *indigni*, we must all offer the prayer at the close of the Church Order of Hippolytus (third century): 'We give Thee thanks because Thou hast imparted to us the reception of Thy holy mystery; let it not be for guilt or condemnation, but for the renewal of soul and body and spirit'.

But the crudities and improprieties to which an intransigeant eucharistic realism can lead here serve to show that *manducatio oralis* is the divisive issue. Here, most noticeably, Calvin cannot go all the way with Luther and later Lutherans. In the chapter which follows we must discuss his eucharistic doctrine and its decisive divergences from the Lutheran tradition. The essential divergence, as we have already noticed, is christological; like Zwingli, he rejects decisively any communication to Christ's human nature of the divine *idiomata* of omnipotence and omnipresence.

This chapter should end, however, with an important issue about which the Reformers were generally agreed. The classic Protestantism of this formative period does not doubt that the Gospel Sacraments are necessary and indispensable. It does not suggest that participation therein is a matter of temperament or inclination. Baptism and Eucharist are integral to the original 'deposit'; to the tradition received of the Lord.

But the Reformers were careful to affirm that the Word could act sacramentally apart from the Gospel Sacraments. In Calvin's memorable words, 'the thief on the cross became the brother of believers though he never partook of the Lord's Supper'. In that sentence you have a statement of fact which is also an appeal to experience; and, as the history of left-wing Protestantism shows, its implications can be far-reaching. But the emphasis of Protestantism being on the 'givenness' of the preached Word and the Sacraments, it affirmed their indissoluble liturgical unity. The Word is luminous and alive at the Holy Table: the Eucharist is always the sacrament of the Word. Because the preaching of the Word—the distinctive liturgical characteristic of the Reformation—was deemed to reach its climax in the Eucharist, frequent celebrations, involving the *full* participation of those present, were strongly advocated. Calvin denounces the medieval custom (for very many people) of communicating once a year only, as an invention of the devil. He asserts that we *may* have daily in the preached and heard Word, in bible-reading and prayer, what the Sacrament gives us: yet not *all* that it gives us, since the Sacrament is God's special and unique testimony to us, and no doublet of what may be had apart from it.

The Lutheran and Reformed traditions are agreed that Sacraments are not an 'extra'. 'No Church can survive', wrote Tillich, 'without the sacramental element.' It is the testimony, in their different ways, of R. W. Dale and C. H. Dodd, that a non-sacramental Christianity tends to become non-supernatural.

Nearly fifty years ago, in an essay on our theme, Barth suggested that Luther was saying 'Yes', and Zwingli 'But'. Because Zwingli tried to do without the 'Yes' he seemed to be saying 'No'. It was Calvin, the man who later said both 'Yes' and 'But', who pointed the way out of a tragic historical cul-de-sac. The chapter which follows is largely devoted to him. (The substance of this concluding paragraph is from *Marburg Revisited*: see p. 8 above.)

BARTLET, J. V. Chapters on patristic christology in *The Lord of Life*, S.C.M.

BAYNES, N. H. *Byzantine Studies*, London, 1955

FRANKS, R. S. *op. cit.* p. 54 above

LIÉBAERT, J. *La doctrine christologique de S. Cyrille d'Alexandrie avant la querelle nestorienne*, Lille, 1951

OSTROGORSKY. *History of the Byzantine State*, Oxford, 1955 (tr. Hussey)

RUNCIMAN, S. *Byzantine Civilization* (Meridian Books)

—— *The Eastern Schism*, Oxford, 1955

SCHOEPS, H. J. *Vom himmlischen Fleisch Christi*, Tübingen, 1951

BRUCE, A. B. *The Humiliation of Christ*, Edinburgh, 1876

SEEBERG, E. *Luthers Theologie: Motive und Ideen* (*Die Gottesanschauung*, p. 182 f.)

EBRARD, E. *Das Dogma vom heiligen Abendmahl und seine Geschichte*, II, 1846

HILDEBRANDT, F. *Est: das lutherische Prinzip*, Göttingen, 1931

KÖHLER, W. *Luther und Zwingli*, I, Leipzig, 1924

—— *Das Religionsgespräch zu Marburg, 1529*, 1929

RUPP, G. *Patterns of Reformation*, Epworth, 1970

MANNING, B. L. *Essays in orthodox dissent*, Independent, 1939

SEEBERG, R. *op. cit.* p. 33 above

IV

LUTHERAN AND REFORMED: THE DISSENSION
OF FIRST COUSINS

i

CALVIN'S 'YES BUT . . .'

'WE affirm that the one Body of Christ, once offered as Victim for our reconciliation with God, is itself offered to us in the Supper.' 'We hold that in the Supper there is a true partaking of the flesh and blood of Christ . . . He is truly offered to us by the Sacraments in order that, being made partakers of him, we may obtain possession of all his blessings; in short, that he may live in us and we in him.'

This is Calvin's frequent and consistent testimony. Christ crucified and risen is given to us *vere et efficaciter* in the Eucharist. The rite conveys what it signifies. Communion with Christ is the dominant fact of Calvin's religion. The Pauline metaphors of being in Christ, and of being crucified with Christ recur constantly in his letters, treatises and commentaries. Nor is there anything passive or indifferent about this communion: it is experienced as living and animating. Calvin borrows a phrase from Luther to insist that the essential Christian experience is not neutral or sluggish: *Christus non otiosus in nobis.*

We have already noticed the affinity of his eucharistic doctrine with that of Luther. Indeed, it was Lutheran criticism (notably Westphal's, from 1552 to 1558) which made him define his doctrine more precisely and with greater clearness. This involved lively controversy, from *Secunda Defensio* to *Ultima Admonitio*, and illustrated the Hindu proverb that there is no hostility like that between first cousins. Niesel has proved that the *Ultima Admonitio* (1557) was not, in fact, Calvin's 'last word', but paragraphs 20 to 34 of the *Institutio* IV. 17, which were carefully worked over before the issue of the definitive edition of 1559. The editors of the great Brunswick edition did not perceive the extent or the significance of Calvin's latest work on these fifteen paragraphs, which are his testament to posterity, so to speak, on the notoriously divisive issue of the real presence. Debate turned mainly on the meaning and implications of the word 'substance'.

(a) Substance

'In the Supper Jesus Christ gives us the very substance (*la propre substance*) of his Body and Blood that we may possess it fully.' What does Calvin mean here by 'substance'? Like all exponents of what happens in sacramental action, he seems to speak with two voices.

On the one hand he defines his meaning repeatedly with all Luther's realism. For example, in his last work on the Eucharist (against Hesshuss, 1561) he writes, 'I do not restrict this union with Christ to union with his divine essence. I say emphatically that it is a union with his flesh and blood; inasmuch as the Gospel did not say "my spirit" but "my flesh" is meat indeed.' Again, 'we say that Christ descends to us as truly by the outward symbol as by his spirit, that he may verily quicken our souls by the substance of his flesh and blood'.

On the other hand, he repeatedly attacks just what such language seems to indicate. He always insists that 'the corporeal presence of Christ' is an 'absurd fiction' if it means that Christ is 'dragged down from heaven' to 'lurk under the covering of the bread'. The localized enclosure of substance (*localis substantiae inclusio*) is strongly repudiated. 'It is enough for us that Christ, out of the substance of his flesh, breathes life into our souls. He diffuses his own life into us, though the flesh itself does not enter us (*in nos non ingrediatur ipsa caro*).'

We should dismiss at once one explanation of this alleged inconsistency; namely that Calvin's occasional 'realism' here was bluff; he was accommodating the Lutherans because of his interest in the contemporary ecumenical movement; he had no real belief in the substantial presence but deliberately obscured the issue with tortuous ambiguities. To anyone who has taken the measure of Calvin's intellectual integrity this sorry hypothesis is not convincing. The only fact which might give it faint plausibility is that Calvin assented both to the Lutheran *Augustana* and to the Swiss *Consensus*. But this indicates, not that his own head was muddled, but that as a good *Unionsmann* he was genuinely anxious to further ecumenical unity.

Ambiguity arose almost inevitably here because of Calvin's use of the same word 'substance' to express two different doctrines: (i) that of the substantial presence of 'Christ with his death and resurrection' in the Eucharist, to which Calvin holds unreservedly; and (ii) that of Christ's Body in the elements, which he rejects as 'this fiction of transfusion'.

Some clarification came out of the resulting controversy, and Calvin elaborated a distinction common to almost all the classic Protestant Confessions. The broken bread and the outpoured wine are signs, but not mere signs (*nuda signa*): sign and substance may not be separated though they must be distinguished. As signs, the bread and wine are instruments signifying, exhibiting, conveying, applying and consummating the redeeming work of Christ. This is what they 'effect' as *signa efficacia*. Speaking of 'substance' in this context, then, Calvin is not concerned with the eternal Son (i.e. the 'person' of the Saviour apart from his 'work'); nor with the 'glorious Body' of the ascended Saviour (i.e. his victory apart from his sufferings and death in the flesh); but with the God–Man of flesh and blood who is *homoousios hemin* (of the same substance as we are), who conjoins us with himself in the communion of his Body, and who feeds and nourishes us with all the benefits of his passion and victory. Communion with Christ—the essential meaning of our salvation—is communion with his whole person, and therefore with his flesh and blood. This is the 'substance' of which all that follows is negative and positive interpretation.

The agreement between Calvin and his Lutheran critics being greater than their disagreement, the debate turned not so much on the reality of the sacrament as on right and wrong ways of defining it. Calvin objected that the Lutheran emphasis on 'is' meant a spatial conjunction of the elements with the

Body and Blood. 'They cannot conceive any other participation of flesh and blood than that which consists either in local conjunction or contact, or in some gross method of enclosing. ... We are bound to hold the presence of Christ in the Supper to be such as neither affixes him to the element of the bread nor encloses him there nor circumscribes him in any way.'

This takes us to the heart of the matter, and to the essential point of difference between the two positions. It may be stated thus. According to the Lutherans there is an immediate spatial relationship between the reality (*res*) and its sign (*signum*). According to Calvin reality and sign are respectively related direct to the believer, whereas between the reality itself and the sign there is only a parallel relationship. If his opponents mean that the reality is inseparable from its sign, Calvin has no great quarrel with them. But this is not their meaning. They may strenuously disavow 'Impanation' (enclosure in bread), but that is what their insistence on spatial conjunction must mean: and Calvin rejects this decisively, not (be it noticed) because it asserts the presence too strongly but because it actually endangers it.

In this contention Calvin is thinking of the Lutheran *manducatio oralis* (partaking with the mouth), on which the issue now begins to turn. Such demolition of Christ's flesh is impossible, since it is 'in heaven'. And, as we shall be noticing in the next chapter, by 'heaven' Calvin does not mean the bright blue sky. His eucharistic theology of communion with the crucified, risen and ascended Saviour presupposes and implies Christian eschatology. It asks the oldest question of all about the goal and final meaning of man's existence: it involves explicit belief about death.

(b) Ascension and Eschatology

The Christ who assumed our flesh and human lot is also the risen and exalted Christ. His bodily ubiquity being axiomatic for the Lutherans, his ascension to the Father has for them a special and somewhat distinctive meaning. He ceases to be conditioned by the physical and moral evil of this fallen world; its finitude, pain and mortality. The words recorded in John 12: 8 refer by implication to the Ascension ('for the poor always ye have with you, but me ye have not always'); but their complete meaning is that Christ will be with his disciples no longer in poverty and humiliation but in power and glory. He is present in this sense in the Eucharist. After his ascension, therefore, he still remains 'bodily' in this our world, albeit in an altered, invisible form of being.

Quite apart from considerations which textual criticism and modern astrophysics now introduce here, this argument (ably presented by Westphal) has obvious force. The eschatology of the New Testament is very largely a 'realized' eschatology, yet it retains some 'futurist' elements: the 'End' which is already here is also not yet here; he who is represented as saying 'Lo I am with you always' is also represented as going away to come again for future judgment. The mysticism expressed in the great Pauline formula 'in Christ', and in so typical a verse as Gal. 2: 20, has always needed some adjustment to the doctrine of the Second Coming.

Calvin rejects Westphal's interpretation of John 12: 8 for two main reasons. First, the exegesis on which it rests is contradicted by the promise of the Holy Spirit, the purpose of which was to meet the sense of loss resulting upon Christ's having left the world. Second, Calvin's understanding of the ascension is Augustinian and scriptural as the Lutheran interpretation in terms of ubiquity is not. For Lutherans the ascension 'on high' is a pictorial expression of Christ's risen sovereignty in all its majesty and glory: the scriptural account of the ascension is a way of describing Christ's invisible presence. As Calvin acutely observes (with a touch of humour?) the Second Coming of Christ must needs be a misnomer for Lutherans, since ultimately it can mean nothing else than that he will again assume visible form.

What, then, does Calvin make of the ascension? The Lutherans complained that his defence of the local as against the illocal interpretation was either rationalism or puerility. But this criticism hardly touches Calvin who (as is shown in Chapter VI) is certainly not thinking mathematically or spatially but biblically and theologically. He believes that, at the ascension, the Body of Christ was exalted 'above all heavens' but he does not thereby commit himself to thinking in terms of bodily presence in a 'place'. (See p. 126 below.)

Though Calvin understands 'the right hand of God' theologically, as an expression of transcendent sovereignty, it is nevertheless a matter of the deepest theological significance for him that Christ's Body, in all its ascended glory, does not cease to be a body (*non tamen verum esse corpus desinit*); and, therefore, is not 'everywhere' but 'in heaven'. This means that he is as much opposed to a false spiritualization as to a false materialization of the 'ascended' Body. It is a Mediator of flesh and blood who, having decisively overcome our world of sin and death, now belongs entirely to the eternal world. This, he says, is the basis of our Christian hope, while the world passeth away and the lusts thereof. This alone is the presupposition of a true Christian eschatology.

Further, Calvin rejects the Lutheran doctrine of the invisible presence of Christ's Body in our world because he finds implicit in it a fourfold threat to this Christian hope.

(i) Since visible corporeality is of the distinctive essence of 'body', the Lutherans are in danger of duplicating Christ's Body with their doctrine of a special divine 'economy' or arrangement whereby it is invisibly present in the Eucharist and yet will appear visibly with Christ at his Coming. (Incidentally, this is one of the rare occasions on which Calvin criticizes Augustine, references to whom abound in his writings. The doctrine of the great *doctor ecclesiae*, that Christ is now visible in heaven but invisible to us in the Eucharist, is here indirectly repudiated by his great disciple. It is ecumenically heartening when the mountain-tops salute one another.)

(ii) There is a threat to Christ's true corporeality, and therefore to his true personality, in this attempt to disrobe his Body of its necessary form. Calvin had not our modern advantages in distinguishing carefully between Hebraic and Greek psychology. Wheeler Robinson, Burton and Pedersen have shown us more accurately what the words *nephesh* and *neshamah*, *basar*, *ruach* and *leb* meant to Israel, and what their Pauline equivalents mean in the New Testament. But Calvin's profound scriptural insight taught him why Christian eschatology is necessarily expressed in terms of the resurrection of the 'body' rather than of a Platonist immortality of the 'soul'. He knew that 'man is an animated body and not an incarnate soul' because scripture had taught him that the body is the real basis of personality.

(iii) The Christian hope of 'bodily' resurrection is menaced, not to say destroyed if Philippians 3:21 means that our bodies will some day be invisible and without dimensional extension, as the glorified Body of Christ is now alleged to be. That passage reads, 'Who shall change our vile body that it may be fashioned like unto his glorious Body'. Calvin's comment upon it here is concerned, as always, with the deepest issues of soteriology: if Christ has *not* taken to the eternal world our true 'bodily' humanity, in which he was born and through which he suffered, then our hope is poverty-stricken and slender indeed. Calvin cannot forget that our hope of 'eternal life' is hope not only of *eternal* life in God, but also of eternal *life*, i.e. that mysterious and miraculous resurrection life which forms a *continuum* with real, human, bodily life in this world.

(iv) His fourth objection might be summed up in the two words *Sursum Corda* (hearts on high). The true differentia of the Eucharist being eschatological rather than mystical, the Lutheran 'invisible presence' tends to divert our attention from Christ himself in heaven to the visible elements on his Table here on earth. Lift up your hearts!

(c) 'Ubiquity' and 'Partaking by the Unworthy'

The basis, if not the ultimate ground, of the difference between the Lutheran and the Reformed theologies of the Eucharist, is the Lutheran doctrine of Christ's bodily ubiquity, already discussed in the previous chapter. We have seen that the key to this difficult doctrine is Luther's distinctive christology; and that Calvin resists the menace of a new Eutychianism which is implicit in it.

He cannot go the whole way with Luther in his understanding of the old patristic formula *'communicatio idiomatum'* (p. 62 above). Of Luther's three interpretations of this mutual interchange, Calvin accepts the first two only (*idiomaticum* and *apotelesmaticum*). He decisively rejects the third because it endangers not only the true humanity but also the true divinity of Christ. *Institutio* II. 14. 2 and IV. 17. 30 are classic statements of his position.

He recognizes the *communicatio idiomatum* in the words of John 3:13 ('and no man hath ascended up to heaven but he that came down from heaven, even the Son of man which is in heaven') with the cautious admission: 'Since Christ, who was true God and true man, shed his blood on the cross for us, the acts performed in his human nature are transferred (improperly yet not without reason) to his divinity'. He added the phrase here bracketed to the edition of 1539. It so far endorses the Lutheran doctrine of ubiquity as to say that Christ the eternal Son is everywhere and therefore 'in heaven'. But Calvin does not admit that Jesus the Son of man was bodily in heaven when uttering the words of John 3:13; there is no real communication of divine characteristics to the human nature.

In short, Christ's human life does *not* share in that divine omnipresence which would nullify its true humanity: and his divinity is not so imprisoned in the human body as to be included therein without remainder, leaving heaven empty. 'I am not ashamed', writes Calvin, 'to quote the trite scholastic distinction, "though the whole Christ is everywhere, not everything which is in him is everywhere"; he is wholly present in the Eucharist, in a special way; for in his flesh he remains in heaven until the Judgment.'

Because Lutherans insisted on Christ's bodily ubiquity they had to insist also on the spatial conjunction of the reality and its sign: as omnipresent, the Body and Blood are 'in, with and under' the bread and wine.

This spatial inclusion inevitably involved the further affirmation that the 'unworthy' at the Lord's Table partake of the Body and Blood, albeit to their deadly hurt. Through his Word and Promise Christ joins his Body and Blood with the bread and wine in closest union: they cannot be disjoined. This is Luther's doctrine in countless contexts. It is formally enunciated in the Schmalkald Articles. The substance of the Supper *is* Christ's Body and Blood, which is received alike by all who partake, even though they be godless, with no faith at all. For mice and men the operation of the Sacrament is uniform.

Here Calvin dissents emphatically. He shares the laudable Lutheran desire to safeguard the objective givenness of the Sacrament, but he may not express this by representing Christ as in communion with those who are far from him. To Lutherans who countered the force of this by saying that Christ exercises his power as Judge (*potestas judiciaria*) over those who receive him unworthily, Calvin puts the acute question: 'how does Christ condemn a man with whom he has entered into communion?' No; the life-giving Food is offered to all, but only believers receive it. The efficacy of the Sacrament presupposes faith.

His opponents represented this as making the efficacy of the rite depend on the attainments and spiritual condition of the participants—a new legalism of faith which would make its 'measure' or 'amount' the essential condition of redeeming grace. Hesshuss actually accused Calvin of the 'sacrilege' which would exclude people of weak or meagre faith from the Lord's Table, and rob fearful and trembling consciences of all assurance. How could they know that they were receiving anything more than empty signs? T. C. Smout's recent account of the working of 'Godly Discipline' in the Kirk (*A History of the Scottish People, 1560–1830*) would suggest that this charge, though actually unfounded, was a shrewd anticipation of later developments. But it was a caricature of Calvin's own position. He affirms that however pitifully feeble one's faith, it may nevertheless be fed and nourished at this Table. As for the 'worthy', they are defined as 'those who come as sick to a Physician; as sinners to the Author of righteousness; as dead to him who makes alive'. Calvin severely rebukes any new gnosticism which would demand a 'perfect' faith: the Supper is intended for the weak and sinful, that they may be helped and their lack of faith and love remedied.

Calvin, then, cannot separate the substance of the Sacrament from its life-giving power: Luther *must* do so because he is logically committed to the participation of the unworthy. Thus, the substance of the Sacrament is identified with the bread and wine by Luther, but with its power by Calvin.

Calvin denies that Christ 'comes down from heaven' into the bread and wine. Using the language of John 6 he speaks of the human nature of Christ, now raised to heavenly glory, as his 'flesh'. This remains in heaven until he comes for judgment (Acts 3: 21). Until then, it can never be present on earth in its substance. Calvin consistently and emphatically denies a transfusion of this substance. But from this 'flesh' in heaven, and through his Spirit (see (d) below), the presence of his Body and Blood is communicated—not to the bread and wine, but to the *souls* of those who believingly partake thereof. This life-giving power is realized principally, though not exclusively (see the closing paragraphs of Chapter III) in the Supper. To summarize this cumbrous exposition as succinctly as possible: in the Reformed tradition, the heavenly substance of the Sacrament is a life-giving power which pours itself from the flesh of Christ in heaven into our souls.

It is here that the famous prepositional formula 'with, in and under' discloses its relevance for the dissensions between Lutheran and Reformed first cousins. For a Lutheran, Christ communicates his Body and Blood not only 'with' the bread, but 'in' it and 'under' it. A Calvinist is happy only with the use of the first of these prepositions since, for him, the real presence means that believing participants receive Christ's Body and Blood, through the Spirit, 'with' the symbols. To put this another way: for a Lutheran, the same physical organ— the mouth—receives both the bread and Christ's Body: for a Calvinist, the Body is received with the 'mouth of the soul'.

Luther's eucharistic doctrine in its completed form from 1528 onwards certainly includes this seeming reversion to earlier ways of thinking. He is saying that what men receive in, with and under the bread and wine is not an *Agens* (active agent) which moves and changes the recipient thereof in certain important ways, but a *Sache* (thing), patient of being sacredly or profanely used by the recipient as he wills. This heavenly *Sache* is so closely bound to the visible elements of the Sacrament by the will and word of Christ that, whenever the rite is celebrated, it cannot be disjoined from them. And because visible elements *are* 'things', such as may be handled worthily or profanely, the heavenly 'thing' *is* subordinated to the human will of anyone who receives it. As Aquinas put it in verse nine of the great Sequence

> *Sumunt boni, sumunt mali*
> *Sorte tamen inaequali*
> *Vitae vel interitus*

(i.e. the evil and the good partake, but the unequal gift is life for these and death for those).

Calvin fears any preoccupation with a 'thing' here, partly because he fears that Christians who have been freed from certain late-medieval superstitions may again be led to worship a created 'thing'; and also because of his lively sense that what is mediated to Christians here is an active, quickening reality. The word which he uses most frequently here is *vivifica* (life-giving, animating).

An old and widely accepted formula for the eucharistic dissensions of Lutherans and Calvinists—that Luther subordinates 'thought' to 'thing', whereas Calvin subordinates 'thing' to 'thought'—equates Calvin with Zwingli's intellectualism too easily to be satisfactory. Ebrard's formula contrasts Luther's *substantia in substantia* (reality as substance) with Calvin's *actus in actu* (reality in action), and is preferable.

For Calvin is saying that this quickening, life-giving reality, which continuously nourishes and increases the spiritual life of men with its hidden efficacy, cannot be received by anyone indifferently; as though it were something provided for the common use of men, like the air we all breathe; but only by those whose heart is opened by faith. It is not possessed by men but it possesses men: it cannot be either well- or ill-used by men, but it moves, stirs and changes men. This power proceeds from the glorified flesh of Christ, and its operation is unceasing; but its special and unique operation is at the Holy Supper.

Leibnitz was anticipating our ecumenical ideal when he wrote that the actual point of agreement between the two great Protestant Confessions is that bodily substance consists in its active and passive power. 'I have read not only Calvin's "Institutes" but also all his other writings in which he treats of the Eucharist; and I have extracted therefrom the passages which prove that this author has seriously, consistently and

85

forcefully taught the real and substantial presence of our Saviour: and when he denies the "real presence" it is indubitable that he does so only when speaking of *une présence dimensionelle*' (*Pensées*: *Oeuvres* V. 211).

(d) The Spirit as 'channel'

Our survey of the divisive eucharistic theology of Protestantism's heroic age began with Calvin's question 'how'. It ends with his answer in terms of the secret power of the Holy Spirit. Christ himself, through that secret power, works upon the spirits of men and imparts to them the heavenly life which proceeds from his glorified flesh. Calvin cites Ephesians 5: 30 as witness that they are thus of Christ's very flesh and bones.

In no part of Calvin's writings is his exposition of the 'real presence' more complete, positive and succinct than in his *Confessio fidei de eucharistia* (1537), a document of less than three hundred words, the importance of which is out of all proportion to its size. (My translation below does little justice to Calvin's concise and elegant Latin, but it tries to give his meaning with fair accuracy.)

All that he says elsewhere of the Holy Spirit as the active link (*vinculum*) and mediating canal or channel (*quidam canalis*) between Christ's heavenly flesh and the believers who feed thereon at his earthly Table, is here summarized. As in the contemporary *Petit Traicté*, and those controversial writings which give final form to the eucharistic theology of the *Institutio*, the Holy Spirit is the means of a two-way traffic, so to speak, whereby Christ descends to us and lifts us to himself. Here is the passage (I use Peter Barth's edition of the *Opera Selecta* I. 435):

> We confess that the spiritual life which Christ imparts to us consists not only in the fact that he quickens us by his Spirit, but that the Spirit also makes us sharers in the power of his life-giving flesh. By this participation we are nourished unto eternal life. When we speak, then, of the communion which believers have with Christ, we mean that they have fellowship no less with his flesh and blood than with his Spirit: it is the whole Christ whom they possess. This, indeed, is the clear witness of Scripture; the flesh and blood of Christ are truly our food and drink. If we seek

life in Christ we have to be thus nourished. For the Apostle is teaching no commonplace or trifling detail when he says that we are flesh of Christ's flesh and bone of his bones: he so designates the extraordinary mystery of our communion with his Body, because no words can sufficiently and worthily explain it.

Further, there is no incompatibility in adding that when our Lord was taken up into heaven, his local presence was taken from us as being no longer requisite here. For, far as we pilgrims of mortality are from the bounds of his habitation, and not included therein, the effective working of his Spirit knows *no* bounds. In this way he links and conjoins us, separated though we are in space and time from one another.

We acknowledge, therefore, that the Spirit links us thus in fellowship with Christ that we may be truly fed for immortality with the substance of the Lord's flesh and blood; and we receive life through our participation therein.

It is this communion of his flesh and blood under the symbols of bread and wine in his sacred Supper that Christ offers and exhibits to all who duly celebrate it, according to his ordinance and institution.

Calvin is saying, then (as the notorious fourth article of the XXXIX Articles of Religion may remind us), that the ascended Christ is separated from us by that infinite distance which distinguishes heaven from earth. But through the activity of the Spirit the ontologically remote is dynamically near. It is so by a twofold operation. Christ comes down to us through the power of the Holy Spirit, and we rise up to the heavenlies through the power of the same Spirit. Thus we are not only linked but united with the heavenly Lord at the eucharistic Feast. 'I say that Christ dwelling in us raises us to himself and transfuses the life-giving vigour of his flesh into us...and again that Christ, while remaining in heaven, descends to us by his power (*virtus*)'. See *Inst.* IV. 17. 16 and *Tracts* ii. 279. 'The Lord's Spirit is the conjoining link which unites us to him: it is a canal, so to speak, through which whatever Christ both is and has is drawn down (*derivatur*) to us.' So, *Inst.* IV. 17. 12.

It cannot be stated too emphatically, or more emphatically than Calvin himself states it, that in speaking of Christ's flesh as *res spiritualis* and of our communion therewith as 'spiritual', Calvin was not speaking metaphorically of something which exists only in our thought. The 'link' in this holy communion is that secret reality beyond our comprehension, the power of the Holy Spirit. It is none other than the third 'person' of the triune Godhead. Calvin rejects the 'cavil' that 'when I say Christ is conceived by faith, I mean that he is conceived only by the imagination and the intellect'. This inmost union with Christ is no mere agreement with his will and an imitation of his virtues! It is, rather, a great mystery (Eph. 5: 32) which is inexpressible by such intellectual and moral categories. Admittedly, this union with Christ is real only for those who seize upon his promises in faith. But though the spiritual partaking of Christ is indeed dependent on faith (from man's side), it is certainly not the same thing as faith. 'For although the Apostle teaches that Christ dwells in our hearts by faith (Eph. 3: 17) no one will interpret him to mean that our faith *is* that indwelling.'

Much, if not all, of this discussion is remote and unreal to the impatient secularism of our post-Christian era—a tissue of scholastic phantasy woven from the exalted scriptural language of Ephesians and the Fourth Gospel. Yet anyone trying to take Christianity seriously will hardly dismiss as irrelevant theological issues which have been the concern of thinkers as competent and diverse as Duns Scotus and Calvin, Petavius and Cheminitz, Leibnitz and Tillich. Admittedly, he will disavow presuppositions and thought-forms of the past which are no longer alive for us. But there are issues which they illustrated which do not die. Indeed, death itself being the final mystery which the meaning of existence involves, eschatology is no peculiar hobby of a few fanatics with nothing more important to do. It is Everyman's conscious or unconscious concern. Eschatologies become dated and discredited, of course; like the supposed prognostications of *Daniel*, *Revelation* or *Old Moore's Almanac*, they become a bore. But the mystery of his mortality is always with man. Calvin's actual categories—like the huge assumption of his age that every statement in Scripture is divinely inspired and infallible—do not now matter very much. There have been several attempts to discover and to state the main constitutive idea in Calvin's whole system:

to find its overall formula or master-key. But if Schulze should be right—that the groundplan of this massive biblical architecture is neither a religious determinism (with double predestination as logical appendage), nor an elaborate ideological preface to Puritanism; but *meditatio futurae vitae* (prolonged thought about life in terms of death)—then, like Stonehenge and the Pyramids, Platonism and Thomism, it is one more monument to *le long espoir et les vastes pensées* of human history. Its dimension is universal. No Christian testimony has more aptly illustrated the confession of the Psalmist: 'He brought me forth into a large place'.

ii

MEDICINE OF IMMORTALITY: THE COMMON WITNESS
OF FATHERS AND REFORMERS

There is a Christian and Catholic universality, too, in Calvin's testimony. At point after point Geneva and Wittenberg are much less out of line with ancient patristic testimony than is commonly supposed.

From its traceable beginnings in the *Didache* the Eucharist has always been the unique expression of the Christian eschatology which is at once 'futurist' and 'realized'. The thought covered by the classic phrases *pharmakon athanasias* (medicine of immortality) and *antidotos tou me apothanein* (antidote to death's poison), and found explicitly in Ignatius, Irenaeus, Tertullian, Cyril of Jerusalem and, above all, in Gregory of Nyssa, appears not infrequently in Calvin, and to a lesser extent in Luther. The Reformers recover something of the ancient patristic insistence that communion with Christ in the Eucharist is not limited to the *anima*, the incorporeal element in man's being: it concerns his physical being also.

With the Hebraic-Christian scriptures as his weapon, Irenaeus counters the Gnostic dualism of spirit and matter as respectively good and evil, by arguing that as the materials of bread and wine in the Eucharist are the very Body and Blood of Christ, the rite invalidates the Gnostic contention, and imparts the medicine of immortality not only to man's spirit but also to his body.

89

Tertullian seems not uninfluenced by the Hebraic genius of Christian psychology as he, too, expounds the indissolubly intimate relation between the corporeal and the incorporeal in man. The physical and the spiritual, here, are distinguishable only in thought. The soul is reached only in and through the body. 'The flesh is washed that the soul may be cleansed from stain; the flesh is anointed that the soul may be hallowed: the flesh is signed with the cross that the soul, too, may be guarded; the flesh is overshadowed by the imposition of hands that the soul, too, may be enlightened by the Spirit; the flesh feeds on the Body and Blood of Christ that the soul, too, may be made full of God' (*On the Resurrection of the flesh, c.viii*).

The sacramental realism of Cyril of Jerusalem (participants in the mysteries of the Eucharist become *sussomoi kai sunaimoi*, i.e. their bodies and blood are one with Christ's Body and Blood) is continued and much developed at the close of the fourth century by Gregory of Nyssa.

A dominant thought in his five chapters which expound the sacraments is that in the gift of the Eucharist the corruption of our bodies is counteracted. The Body which has triumphed victoriously over Death is here communicated to our decaying mortal bodies. The Eucharist extends the Incarnation; it is therefore antidote to poison and medicine for our eating. It 'makes over' and 'changes over' our corrupt and mortal humanity into itself. In Gregory of Nyssa this 'medicinal', 'divinizing' virtue of the Eucharist finds its most articulate expression. As in baptism the soul is united to God, so the whole force of the Eucharist is directed to the bodies of men. We have noticed in the previous chapter that this 'laboratory' conception of soteriology is characteristic of Greek Orthodoxy. The Eucharist is an 'extension of the Incarnation' in the special sense that it gives effect to that deification (*theopoiesis*) of our corrupt and mortal human nature through the union of the Incarnate Word with humanity.

At first sight, it might seem that Luther, as the greatest of the graecizing Westerns (p. 68 above), is obviously cast for the role of Protestantism's Gregory of Nyssa. Arguing that Christ's flesh in the Eucharist does not undergo the normal processes of disintegration because it is not 'corruptible food', he says: 'corruptible food is transformed into the body which consumes it, whereas this Food transforms the body which consumes it into Itself; making it like Itself, spiritually alive and eternal ... This poor worm-bag (*Madensack*), our body, thus receives the hope of resurrection from the dead, and eternal life. All that is carnal in it must become spiritual as it partakes of this spiritual Food. As St. Paul says in 1 Cor. 15:44 "it is raised a spiritual body"' (*Dass diese Worte* ... W.A. xxiii. 203, 205).

Again at the Marburg Colloquy he is reported as saying: 'the Body of Christ feeds man's body for eternity (*aeternaliter*); as the mouth receives the Body, it acquires a certain immortality (*quandam immortalitatem*)'.

But there are difficulties about this evidence. The first passage comes from the notoriously polemical manifesto of 1527 and is not, strictly speaking, typical of Luther's writings taken as a whole. The second comes from rough notes made by Zwingli's friends, Collin and Hedio, during the Colloquy. These, as Erichson observes (in W.A. xxx. iii. 112–21) are verbally much alike. Did they compare and adjust their notes in the evenings, or on the way home?

The great authority of Walter Köhler's *Luther und Zwingli* (I. 642) and his brilliant pamphlet *Das Religionsgespräch zu Marburg 1529* confirm the importance of these details. For, by an ironical paradox, they mean that whereas Calvin's references to the 'medicine of immortality' or its equivalent are not infrequent, Luther's use of the whole concept covered by this and similar patristic language is limited to his very polemical mood before and at Marburg, when he is arguing *gumnastikōs* (to use Origen's word), i.e. 'stripped for the fight'. The decisive evidence is that this line of thought is entirely ignored by Luther in his *Great Catechism* of the same year (1529); nor does it reappear in any of his later eucharistic writings; nor do the confessional Statements and Symbols of later Lutheranism refer to it.

The real difficulty is discussed with learning and sympathy by Julius Müller in his *Vergleichung der Lehren Luthers und Calvins vom heiligen Abendmahl* (*Dogmatische Abhandlungen*, pp. 404 ff.). He observes, rightly that from 1527–29 Luther *does* ascribe to the Lord's Supper a new function in relation to the resurrection of the body. 'The unconscious body doesn't know that it is eating food whereby it is to live eternally: but the soul sees and understands that the body must live eternally because it partakes of an eternal Food which will not leave it in the grave to see corruption.' But Müller rightly adds that, as it stands, this is not strictly scriptural. To interpret John 6: 54 *only* of the Sacrament is inadmissible. Further, scripture promises eternal life not to those who partake of this Sacrament but to all who believe (John 3: 16 and 6: 40, 47). The Holy Spirit who renews us inwardly through faith and unites us to Christ, is scripture's most certain pledge for our future salvation (as in Rom. 8: 11; Eph. 1: 13–14, 4: 30).

In the judgment of this fine dogmatic theologian who 'wears so well' (as Reinhold Niebuhr once said to me when reading me his manuscript on *Man as Sinner* for his forthcoming Gifford Lectures), Luther thought more correctly when, as in the fifth section of the *Great Catechism*, he thought more calmly: 'one must regard the Sacrament . . . simply as healing, comforting medicine (*Arzenei*) which helps us and gives life both to soul and body. For to heal the soul is also to help the body'.

Calvin doubtless agreed with this latter statement. For it is his sober and consistent thought from 1536 onwards that the efficacy of the real presence is such that it not only brings an unshakeable confidence of eternal life to our souls but also makes us sure of the immortality of our 'flesh', since our 'flesh' is already quickened by his immortal flesh and, as it were (*quodammodo*), shares in its immortality (OS. I. 143). 'I do not deny', says Calvin, 'that our flesh is refreshed by that spiritual meat and drink. For we have communion with Christ in the hope of a blessed resurrection, and therefore we must be one with him not in soul only but in flesh (*non anima solum sed carne etiam in ipsum coalescere necesse est*)' (Tracts II. 436).

Calvin recalls the ancient patristic witness, too, in that his eucharistic theology is always dynamic. Christ is not present because his Body is 'located' in the elements, but because the

Spirit makes it effectively ours, enabling us by faith to enter into communion with Christ crucified and risen. By faith, too, we transcend time at the Holy Table, and in our oneness with Christ we overstep not only the historical but also the eschatological boundary. Here we are one with the Christ who broke bread and poured out wine in the upper room, and with the same Christ who will feast with his saints in the messianic kingdom. Thus, the meaning of the Eucharist is not tied to the moment of our participation therein: 'assuredly if there be not a perpetual communion beyond the act of communicating, nothing more will be conferred than the remembrance of something lost (as soon as we withdraw from the Table). The Lord affirms his perpetual abiding with us, sealing it in the Supper. The communion of which we are partakers at the Supper is perpetual' (Tracts I. 470). Like the fifth article of the Genevan Catechism, the Scots Confession of 1560 makes the same point: 'We affirm that the faithful in the right use of the Lord's Table, have such conjunction with Christ Jesus as the natural man cannot comprehend; yea, and further we affirm that albeit the faithful oppressed by negligence and manlie infirmity do not profit so much as they would at the very instant action of the Supper, yet it shall after bring forth fruit as lively seed sown in good ground; for the Holy Spirit which can never be divided from the right institution of the Lord Jesus will not frustrate the faithful of the fruit of that mystical union.'

Luther ends his *Babylonish Captivity* on the same note of 'realized eschatology'; strengthened by the sacrament we pass out of the world as men 'born into a new and eternal life and destined to eat with Christ in the kingdom of his Father . . . Thus it is evident that Christ instituted the sacrament of the bread that we might receive the life which is to come.' For all the Reformers, 'realized eschatology' at the Supper necessarily involves fellowship and brotherly love among the communicants who are thus knit together into the One Body. As Calvin put it: we are mutually bound one to the other in all the obligations of love.

Once again, we come back from this rarefied atmosphere of dogmatic space-travel to the multitudes of modern men and women for whom, in comparison with the technological realities of secular experience, this theological speculation is boring, meaningless or incredible. This entirely intelligible attitude is taken, for example, by a highly civilized but not untypical modern man, Leonard Woolf, in the first volume of his five-volume autobiography. For many a modern man and woman the death of a human individual registers his end: his extinction. Mortal man may live on, so to speak, in a collective, racial sense: this obvious fact has stimulated Comte's historic imagination, and in George Eliot's *Choir Invisible* it has been preached with noble earnestness as a supreme opportunity of serving mankind. (The sheer pessimism of its ultimate implications has received devastating criticism from Berdyaev.) Even this interpretation of personal survival is limited to the unknown time-span of humanity's life on this planet; or to that mythological End-of-all-things when the wide firmament is rolled up like a scroll and the aeons are no more.

Today the Christian believer respects this unbelief as understandable, but for him it is irrelevant. He sees the ultimate meaning of human existence differently. He believes in the living and eternal God. This belief is neither provable nor rationally demonstrable, but it has determinate meaning. It is a faith which is also a hope. In every generation it has commended itself to all sorts and conditions of men, and constrained their willing allegiance. Nominal Christianity apart, from the beginning they have known 'joy and peace in believing'. All that they can say today is all that the disciple of Christ has ever been able to say: 'he that hath ears to hear, let him hear'; 'Lord I believe; help thou mine unbelief.'

The essential affirmations and deepest insights of this Christian faith may be an illusion: to deny this abstract possibility would be to assume infallibility. It is undeniable, too, that they may be true. And the affirmation which is integral to this faith and cannot be taken away from it without destroying its historic identity and turning it into something different—is eternal life in the God and Father of our Lord Jesus Christ. For Christians, death is not extinction. They do not pretend to be able to define either eternity or time. They know nothing about the undiscovered country beyond death.

All their thought about it is what the imagination bodies forth. Here they are following darkness like a dream. But what they know is the Light that has gone before them.

The resurrection of the 'body' rather than the immortality of the 'soul' has always been the authentic Christian expression of this hope. We know nothing whatever about a disembodied personal existence. (See p. 80 above.) The body, despite those replacement-changes which take place within it every few years, is the organic 'continuum' which is the basic expression of our continuous psycho-physical identity from womb and cradle to senility, death and the grave. At death this empirical body *is* destroyed, in crematorium, grave or wherever. But it is the Christian faith that the God and Father of our Lord Jesus Christ will continue the life that he has given and taken away, in the sheer miracle of resurrection. We know no more: we believe no less.

The Reformers, like the Fathers, did not evade the issues which this stupendous faith involves. They stuck their necks out. They grappled with the difficulties imposed upon them by a sacrosanct text of Scripture. They are hardly to be blamed for their scholastic *credenda* which have burdened the people of God in one generation after another, and which have more often defeated than served the divine purpose.

The next two chapters will suggest that we need not, and *may* not allow ourselves to be bound by their apologetic methods which are now dated and, in some respects, discredited. We no longer think as they did about Scripture as verbally inerrant because divinely inspired. All that matters is faith in the grace and truth which came by Jesus Christ. For a Christian that is everything.

SHORT BIBLIOGRAPHY

CALVIN. *Institutes* (Calvin Translation Society), 1845
—— *Calvini Opera Selecta*, ed. P. Barth and W. Niesel, I, III–V, Munich, 1925
—— *Confessio fidei de eucharistia* (1537), *Op. Sel.* I. 435

CALVIN. *Libellus de Coena Domini* (1541), i.e. *Petit Traicté*, *Op. Sel.* I. 503 f.
—— *Tracts* (Calvin Translation Society), vol. II
NIESEL, W. *Calvins Lehre vom Abendmahl*, Munich, 1935
MÜLLER, J. *Vergleichung der Lehren Luthers und Calvins vom heiligen Abendmahl* (in his *Dogmatische Abhandlungen*, 1870)
IMBART DE LA TOUR, P. *Les Origines de la Réforme*, Paris, 1935
Tome IV, *Calvin et l'Institution Chrétienne*
EMPIE, P. C. and MC. CORD, J. I. (editors). *Marburg Revisited*, 1966
TILLICH, P. *The Protestant Era*, Chicago, 1948
SMOUT, T. C. *A History of the Scottish People*, 1560–1830, Collins, 1969
DODD, C. H. *New Testament Studies*, Scribners, 1952
No. vii, *The Communion of Saints* (Ingersoll Lecture), 1935
No. viii, *Eternal Life* (Ingersoll Lecture), 1950

V

ATHENS AND JERUSALEM: THE DUAL HERITAGE

i

TERTULLIAN'S CERTAIN IMPOSSIBILITY

IT may have been my new bi-focals; but the title which caught my eye in some religious journal seemed to read 'Should Christians think?' This was surprising, not to say preposterous; so I looked more closely, to discover that the correct reading was 'Should Christians drink?' I was reassured: for whether we should drink or not, it is surely indisputable that we should serve God with all our mind. Thinking is our business.

How surprising it is, then, that some of the greatest Christian thinkers throughout nineteen centuries seem to have insisted that thinking is not our business.

There was Tertullian's notorious outburst at the end of the second century, 'What has Athens to do with Jerusalem; the Academy with the Church?' And this brilliant North African apologist for the emerging Catholic orthodoxy of the West himself answered his question, saying 'The pupil of Hellas has nothing in common with the pupil of Heaven'. Tertullian rails against Aristotle, 'unhappy Aristotle' as he calls him; and says that in the presence of the evangel all philosophical enquiry is irrelevant, and worse: the search for truth is a confession of apostasy.

Again, Luther's attacks on Reason as 'the Devil's Bride', 'the Harlot', 'the Fool', show a like extravagance. He, too, abuses Aristotle who, since the century of Aquinas and Dante, had come to be revered by Christendom as *the* philosopher, 'the master of them that know'. Luther felt that it was outrageous to give pre-eminence to 'that monster', 'that blind heathen'. Scholastic theologians might clinch their debating points with some *ipse dixit* of the great Master, but Luther's short answer to that was 'the Holy Ghost is greater than Aristotle'.

Again, Pascal was one of the creative mathematicians of the seventeenth century. I need not remind you that his most famous book is entitled 'Thinking' (*Pensées*). Yet the clue to his life was that *Memorial* written on parchment one night, sewn within the lining of his coat, and discovered there after his death. It contained the famous words, 'God of Abraham, Isaac and Jacob; not of the thinkers and intellectuals'.

Then there is Kierkegaard, the Dane whose importance we have taken a hundred years to recognize. Not only did he repudiate Hegel's cool contention that Christianity is essentially philosophy, anything else in it being an expendable superfluity; he made a complete break with the philosophical theology which involves a theoretical or speculative attitude towards the divine; faith in God is neither inference nor hypothesis; it rests on decision, made in response to revelation.

Again, Dean Mansel of St. Paul's is remembered because of his Bampton lectures in 1858 entitled *The Limits of Religious Thought*. He argued that, as all human knowledge is limited to the finite, a conception of God is self-contradictory. All conception is a limitation; and a limitation of the illimitable is not only impossible but meaningless. Religious thought can be no more than regulative of our practice.

Finally there is our contemporary, Karl Barth, for whom the genius of Christian theology is expressible only in biblical categories and symbols. Since the eternal God is 'altogether other' than finite man, any human comprehension of God's transcendent otherness is an impossibility. Indeed, it is no better than idolatry. The Christian knowledge of God comes only as revelation from the Beyond. It is sheer gift; a bolt from the blue.

How are we to make sense of this anti-intellectual emphasis—this separation of biblical sheep from philosophical goats, which recurs constantly in the long history of Christian theology? An obvious difficulty is that those who repudiate thought in this way are themselves very effective thinkers. It is to Tertullian that the dogmatic theology of the Latin West owes much of its terminology, its precise definition, its scholastic form: his great work *Against Praxeas* has strongly influenced subsequent Christian thought. Luther, too, was a competent and acute scholastic, as his subtle treatises on the Real Presence sufficiently indicate. Again, Pascal was himself a notable illustration of his famous definition of Man, 'not only a reed, the weakest in nature, but a thinking reed [*roseau pensant*]'. And Kierkegaard was certainly not hostile to philosophy as such: he owed nothing to Rousseau's romantic nonsense about the 'noble savage'—the Rousseau who had actually written that a thinking man is an animal gone bad (*un homme qui médite est un animal dépravé*). As for Dean Mansel, he was a professional philosopher, the author of treatises on metaphysics and logic. And Karl Barth? Well, his son Professor Marcus Barth said to me with a charming chuckle some little time ago in Chicago, 'Do not make any mistake. My father has the works of Aquinas, Kant and Schleiermacher within easy reach of his desk, and he often consults them!'

The difficulty, then, is formidable. Moreover the easy solution which suggests itself must be ruled out at once. I mean that we may not belittle or dismiss all this as something peculiar to these men. So far from being unusual or exceptional, this emphatic distinction between reason and revelation—between *scire* and *credere*—is a recurrent theme of Christian doctrine from, say, Justin Martyr in the second century to Ritschl in the nineteenth. Aquinas himself, whose *Summa* fuses biblical revelation with Aristotelian philosophy and is Rome's authoritative exposition of faith as an intellectual virtue—even he stiffly maintains that the supreme doctrines of Christianity—the Incarnation and the Trinity—are intrinsically inaccessible to human comprehension and reason. Let me add that precisely the same stand is taken by that Aquinas of Anglicanism, perhaps the finest mind of the sixteenth century, Richard Hooker.

Very well; since reason, human enquiry as such, is certainly not repudiated by Christendom's classic apologists, why are they thus ranged against Athens in the name of Jerusalem? I submit that the answer lies in two facts of which the Christian Church is the undying embodiment.

(i) The first fact is that this Christian knowledge of God does come to humanity in terms of action rather than of thought. It is concerned with historic actuality rather than with abstract ideas; with good news rather than with good notions. Its context is a sequence of events in time—what scripture knows as the 'mighty acts' of God. The God of the Hebraic Christian Gospel is, as Luther saw, *deus actuosus*, i.e. he is known for what he is by what he does: and what he does is to make for himself a people, the 'people of God'. Christianity is not a set of timeless intellectual truths: it is common life, new and unique, lived in God: it authenticates itself in terms of historic happenings: its kerugmatic spearhead is a uniquely revelatory and redemptive event, Jesus Christ. The Church is his 'Body'. It is the continuing expression and communication of this Gospel of divine action, given to humanity in terms of Exodus and Sinai, Bethlehem and Calvary, Easter and Pentecost, and made presently real in the time-sacrament of the Christian Year. But the point is that this revealing actuality is not anything which your philosopher might have excogitated 'within the bounds of pure reason'. Neither Platonist nor Aristotelian could say, or would want to say, that the eternal Ground of all Being is personal, holy and loving: that at a point in historic time 'he' took flesh and dwelt among us, suffered and died; and that his dying on the Tree is glorious for ever with the power of redeeming love. To men of Athens, philosophical minds in every generation, such a paradox is foolishness; but because it is actualized in the ongoing life of the Body of Christ, sons of Zion have never been lacking to proclaim it.

(ii) That word 'paradox' brings us to the second fact, constitutive and distinctive of the Gospel, which is that this revelation of God in the man Jesus *is* inherently paradoxical. We have only to look at the Christian Faith's classic definition of itself in the Creed to realize that it has three great 'moments'— Incarnation, Crucifixion and Resurrection—in each of which this theological paradox is inescapable.

(a) Incarnation, God in the flesh, is necessarily paradoxical if it be true at all. It cannot be stated without involving logical contradiction. The Infinite in the finite: the Eternal in the temporal: the divine Logos, God's very Self, becoming human: divine 'nature' and human 'nature' in one person—this whole christological paradox is absurd on the presuppositions of Athens. For, in the thought of the Greeks from, say, Plato to Plotinus, the divine is by definition infinite, eternal, illimitable, unchangeable, incorruptible, impassible. To say, therefore, that the divine became incarnate, that the impassible suffered, that the immortal died, is not only paradoxical but absurd. Yet it is just this paradox, this 'coincidence of opposites', which all christological confessions—ancient and modern, eastern and western, catholic and protestant—are always striving to vindicate convincingly, to articulate intelligibly, in creed and hymn, dogma and sacrament, liturgy and art.

When Gregory of Nyssa writes that the incarnate Logos *apathōs epathen*, i.e. was impassibly passible; suffered without suffering; when Luther exclaims 'God is this Man; this Man is God'; when John Donne's sonnet for Christmas Eve thus addresses the Virgin,

> Immensity cloistered in thy deare wombe
> Now leaves His well-beloved imprisonment:

when the same coincidence of opposites appears in Isaac Watts,

> Our souls adore the eternal God
> Who condescended to be born:

or when Charles Wesley takes this paradox to the very cliff-edge of patripassian heresy in that verse of adoring gratitude to 'Jehovah crucified'—in all this you have testimony to the paradox necessarily inherent in the religion of the Incarnation, and to the absurdity of thinking of it logically. Here Jerusalem ignores the disciplined metaphysics of Athens, as it must do, if the witness on every page of the New Testament, that 'God was in Christ', is to be bodied forth in human concepts at all. Further, the juxtaposed opposites of its christological language do not resolve the inescapable paradox: they neither try to do so nor claim to do so—not even in the Definition of Chalcedon nor in the so-called Athanasian Creed. They leave the paradox as such. The Church is enduring testimony that its religion exists in its own right, uses its own distinctive

101

language and is its own interpreter. The Church's basic presupposition is this paradox of 'God is the flesh'. As Isaac Watts put it,

> Where reason fails with all her powers,
> There faith prevails and love adores.

(b) Crucifixion. This is the second great paradoxical moment, namely that the Incarnate One, the Christ, died for our sins: that is, the paradox of grace, the wonder of divine forgiveness and redemption. The holy One, whose holy Law is the only true structure for human life, and whose judgment is no silly fable—he nevertheless loves us sinners with an everlasting love. But it is precisely the heights and depths of this huge paradox—that 'God justifies the ungodly'—which altogether transcend the moralistic logic of human reason. And so *this* too, this Hebraic-Christian dialectic of No and Yes, is to the Greeks foolishness. The declaration that the creator and judge of all the earth loves, forgives and redeems his rebel creation, *is* absurd to the legalistic wisdom of this world, and to the distributive justice of its law-courts and prisons, its judges and executioners. Luther saw that whenever this paradox, so offensive to our tidy moralistic logic, is got rid of, and some calculus of rewards and penalties put in its place, the essential genius of the Good News of redeeming grace is betrayed, and its historic identity lost. A righteous God, of purer eyes than to behold iniquity, who nevertheless yearns after sinners in love, giving himself for them to the uttermost—this is unintelligible to reason and to the justice of the law court. It is, as Luther put it, 'against all reason'. To the eminent English jurist Sir James Stephen it is not only against all reason: it is wrong. You may remember that he pronounced the Sermon on the Mount 'not only imprudent but unjust'. His presuppositions were exclusively legal. But Luther's presuppositions are both legal and evangelical. He is wrestling with a paradox alien to the logic of legal process; namely that the judgment of the moral law and the grace of forgiveness are *both* divine. The jurist rejects the logical incompatibility: Luther accepts it and lives with it. *Gottes Wort wider Gottes Wort laut.* There happens to be an exact translation of this in

Shakespeare: 'The Word itself against the Word' (*Richard the Second*, V. 5).

And so the sheer wonder of redeeming grace cannot be expressed save in the great evangelical antinomies: Law and Gospel; Judgment and Mercy; Wrath and Love; No and Yes; 'Depart from Me' and 'Come unto Me'. The vital point, again, is that the Church is the home of these antinomies; not the Academy. I mean that the paradox is not resolved academically by any scholastic rationale or any formal scheme of atonement. The paradox is left as such. It becomes intelligible and precious in the Church, where the people of God live with its irresolvable tensions and antinomies; where they *kneel down* before the Five Wounds. *The Hymns for the Use of the People called Methodists* mean just this.

(c) Resurrection is the third paradoxical moment, the climax of these irresolvable antinomies at the heart of the historic faith of Christendom. *Credo resurrectionem.* It is a credal declaration that our historical existence, annihilated in crematorium or grave, is nevertheless consummated beyond history. But this lies beyond the limit of anything thinkable or conceivable. A redeemed and recreated order of existence, beyond death and time, is beyond all knowledge and all thought. What can reason have to say here? As Tillich observes, even Plato makes Socrates put a question mark against the very arguments for the immortality of the soul which he develops in the discussion prior to his death.

Well, Jerusalem lives with the paradox, the No of death and the Yes of resurrection unto life eternal. The No is the stark, empirical universality of death—'all men are mortal'; 'stone dead hath no fellow'; 'in Adam all die'. The Yes is faith's victory over the last enemy—'the sounding of trumpets on the other side'; 'in Christ shall all be made alive'. The Church is the context wherein men resolve the paradox by living it. In Luther's moving epigram, *unter und über dem Nein, das tiefe heimliche Ja* (deeper and higher than the No, the deep mysterious Yes).

It is against this triple paradoxical background that an epigram of Tertullian's, often misquoted, should be understood. Let me quote it correctly and in its context. 'The Son of God was born: I am not ashamed of it, for it is shameful. The Son of God died: it is credible for the very reason that it is silly. The Son of God, having been buried, rose again: it is certain because it is impossible' (*de carne Christi*, v).

These notorious words state extravagantly and truculently the paradoxical faith which the Church exists to embody. And here the famous question has obvious relevance. The apologist who can cry 'It is certain because it is impossible' is, not surprisingly, the rhetorician who can ask the contemptuous question, 'What has Athens to do with Jerusalem; the Academy with the Church?'

ii

THE 'IMPREGNABLE ROCK OF HOLY SCRIPTURE'
AND MODERN INSIGHTS

But just here serious difficulties present themselves. They come, with fitting irony, from the Academy; and today even a Tertullian has to face them.

'It is certain.' But is it? Those factual certainties—his birth and life, his words and works, his passion and death, his resurrection and ascension—do they include no uncertain elements? Is the total scriptural authentication of the revelatory Event the 'impregnable rock' which Mr. Gladstone declared it to be?

All the religious disquiet of our age is bound up with that question. It brings us at one bound to the contemporary world of scientific and historical investigation, with its staggering enlargements of our knowledge. Ours is the world, not only of Darwin, Freud and Einstein, but also of Wellhausen and Bultmann, of archaeology and Carbon-14 dating. 'It is certain' was Tertullian's shrill decision. Is it? In what sense?

Up to the eighteenth century such a question hardly arose. In Catholic and Protestant Christendom alike, the truth of every biblical statement was taken for granted. Scripture was 'holy' scripture because, quite literally and unambiguously, God was its author. The four evangelists, like the prophets before them, were *amanuenses Spiritus sancti*: that is, they wrote at God's dictation: hence their sacred infallibility.

But informed Christian apologetic has long been retreating from a position which, now more than ever, is indefensible. The venerable dogma of the verbal inerrancy of Scripture just dies in our mouths. For since that Scripture is essentially historical, it can no more escape the microscopic scrutiny of historical research as we now know it, than can Livy or Plutarch. Indeed, the enormous scientific toil dedicated to this research during the past hundred years is one of the great chapters in the history of Christianity. Speaking broadly, it is a chapter which records three momentous discoveries. It has given us more or less successively, three new and revolutionary insights into the nature and meaning of holy scripture.

(i) The first is the relativism implicit in modern historical and archaeological study. I mean that the steady enlargement of modern man's vision of the ancient past constantly compels him to see as relative much that traditional piety revered as absolute and unique. This is now so familiar that I may do no more than mention three relevant examples from the field of archaeology.

A century ago ancient clay tablets were discovered, a Babylonian version of the stories of the Creation and the Flood; the crudely mythological original of the version which became demythologized and refined much later in the opening chapters of *Genesis*. This was disturbing (to say the least!) to the classic Christian dogma that scripture has the uniqueness of divine dictation.

Again, the Code of Hammurabi discovered at Susa some seventy years ago was a corpus of Babylonian law, much older than the Mosaic law of the Pentateuch, yet resembling it so closely that some influence, direct or indirect, is indubitable. Here again, Jews and Christians could no longer assert *simpliciter* that Moses had received the sacred Law 'brand new from heaven', so to speak. Are the Ten Commandments uniquely sacred then? Are they not just Semitic?

Again, those ancient Canaanite poems on the tablets discovered at Ras Shamrah in N. Syria are closely parallel in metrical form, language and liturgical symbolism with several Old Testament psalms traditionally attributed to David. Now there are good Christians in Scotland, affectionately known as

'Wee Frees', who distinguish firmly between 'human' hymns (which they don't sing) and the psalms of David (which they do). But research on sacral kingship in ancient Israel, notably that by Professor Aubrey Johnson of Cardiff, has shown that the 'royal' or 'enthronement' psalms are almost certainly Hebrew adaptations of those older Ugaritic poems: that is, they are in part a legacy of Canaanite mythology which is not only human but heathen.

I am aware, of course, that the past means what it has come to mean; that values are not prejudiced by origins; that 'origins or pedigrees have . . . little bearing upon truth' (Karl Popper). But I cite the foregoing familiar facts because they illustrate from the field of biblical archaeology modern man's greatly enhanced awareness of the variety and the relatedness of his past. Those cave-frescoes in the valley of the Dordogne, drawn by pathetic human hands some thirty thousand (30,000) years ago, are almost overwhelming reminders of the immense age of our humanity: that our world is a huge museum with many more rooms in it than Tertullian or Mr. Gladstone could possibly know of.

In short, the relativity of much that once seemed absolute and alone normative is the first of the three main discoveries which modern critical historicism has made in the field of biblical study.

(ii) The second is source-analysis, and what it discloses about the way scripture understands, interprets and transmits human history.

In the Old Testament that history, which our fathers took to be factual truth infallibly authenticated, is really the complex resultant of a long redactional or editorial process, the editors being Time and impassioned Memory, Suffering and national Disaster, and a living Belief in the living God. The actual past, lost in legendary mists, becomes a past informed and transformed by religious faith. The Exodus, for example, *was* an historical event: the Hebrews did escape from Egypt even though no Egyptian records corroborate it. But the Rabbis who put the Old Testament into its present shape see it as Israel's supreme experience of the gracious purpose of God. Here interpreting myth is much more important than bare historical event. Here, history (*Geschichte*) is redemptive history (*Heilsgeschichte*): the sacred traditions of the past reach their canonical literary form after being controlled and interpreted, shaped and embroidered, by Israel's enduring faith. As Güthe put it some eighty years ago in the *Geschichte des Volks Israel*, 'the object of the narrators is not to relate what actually happened, but to shape traditions of the past for the good of the present'. In short, the history presented in the Old Testament is *Redaktionsgeschichte* just because it has been seen throughout as *Heilsgeschichte*.

What of source-analysis in the New Testament? Here, too, the Gospel story came to be recorded by processes different from those presupposed by traditional piety. That piety, by the way, was not quite consistent. The Bible being its infallible Book, the complete and final speech of God, the four Gospels were (if one may so put it!) *equally* infallible. But, in fact, Matthew was Christendom's favourite, and Mark was regarded as Matthew's *pedisequus et breviator*: that is, Mark was a copy and abridgement of Matthew, a sort of poor relation. But in 1835, a momentous date in modern biblical study, Karl Lachmann formulated and virtually solved what is known as the synoptic problem. As is well known, his lasting achievement was twofold: first, he demonstrated the priority of Mark; second, he set out the Two-Source theory which, details apart, is now almost universally accepted. That is, Mark was the foundation-document which Matthew and Luke each incorporated, with considerable editorial modifications, into their respective gospels. In addition, they used a second common source, now labelled Q, consisting almost entirely of sayings of Jesus. Each incorporated this second source in his own way, rearranging and altering details with no little editorial freedom.

This freedom went so much further in the latest and greatest of the gospels, which traditionally bears the name of John, that the result was something different in *kind* from the other three. And here the critical scholarship of the nineteenth century developed that of the third. For it was Clement of Alexandria in the early third century who wrote that John had composed a spiritual gospel in contrast to the bodily facts which the earlier gospels had set forth: and his great contemporary Origen, with the reckless honesty characteristic of him, wrote explicitly that here 'spiritual truth is preserved in what one might call corporeal falsehood'. The kernel of truth is preserved within the husk of fiction.

Well, the Fourth Gospel *is* theological rather than historical in its purpose and final meaning. It does use history with sovereign freedom as the vehicle of transcendental ideas. In chapters 14 to 17 the unknown author sets his own meditative discourses on the lips of the Messiah. They are his exposition of the New Exodus, during the New Passover: they are the 'johannine' interpretation of the Christian Eucharist. None of the evangelists are mere chroniclers; but this evangelist is supremely the profound, meditative artist, for whom the story of the Man of Nazareth can be truly understood only in terms of the incarnate Logos or Word, who has descended from heaven and will return thither. The seven great Signs, beginning with the water and the wine at Cana, and reaching their climax in the raising of Lazarus, are unknown to the 'synoptics': they are the 'johannine' way of declaring the divine glory of the Messiah. These Signs are concerned with *Wahrheit* rather than with *Wirklichkeit*: they testify not to actuality but to Reality.

Critical analysis of the gospels in the nineteenth century concluded, then, that in Mark we are nearest to historic fact, theological interpretation being at a minimum; whereas, in 'John', even what is presented ostensibly as historic fact is largely if not wholly theological interpretation. Biblical studies in the twentieth century have not invalidated this broad, general conclusion, but they have seriously modified it: too sharp an antithesis between 'synoptic' and 'johannine' is now disallowed. In his second great volume on the Fourth Gospel, Professor C. H. Dodd demonstrates that there is more use of authentic historical tradition in that gospel than had been supposed: further, we now realize that the Synoptics, notably Mark, are much less 'synoptic' (in the nineteenth-century meaning of this word) and much more theological than had been supposed. Indeed, during the past forty years we have come to see that *all* the gospels, and not just the latest, are primarily confessional and theological in purpose, rather than biographical and historical in our modern sense.

In short, source-analysis has shown that biblical history (like all history) is in some sense *Redaktionsgeschichte*. It discloses large subjectivist elements in that historical witness of the Bible which was traditionally revered as objective and sacrosanct. This is the second great insight which critical historicism has given to biblical study.

(iii) The third is the disclosure by form-analysis that the gospels are not so much sources for a life of Jesus as products and embodiments of the life and witness of the early Church. Form-analysis seeks to go behind source-analysis by penetrating that obscure period between A.D. 30 and 65 when memories and traditions of what the Lord said and did circulated orally and were not yet written. It attempts to classify the recognizable forms and patterns into which this oral tradition gradually crystallized through constant repetition, especially in assemblies for worship.

Pre-literary analysis of this kind is no novelty of course. It is used in the study of the earliest forms of Roman Law. Dodd observes that it has been fruitfully applied to various folk-traditions—German, Russian, Irish and Welsh—and to the history of the New Zealand Maoris which rests entirely on oral tradition. But, as applied to primitive Christian tradition, form-analysis discloses something which can be as disturbing as it is surprising to us. We pride ourselves on what we hope and believe to be our disinterested use of the historical method. We like to think that we reverence historic fact as something not to be tampered with. We feel that historiography must be strictly conditioned by evidence. It seems, however, that the earliest traditions about the Lord Jesus were not only used, but were sometimes manipulated, to meet the emerging needs of the Church in all their variety and urgency. The Church early found itself facing problems—missionary, ethical, catechetical, liturgical and polemical problems: and so the floating, oral tradition about Jesus was not as rigid and static as we might have expected it to be, but plastic and patient of change. It was not only used to meet varying situations: it was itself coloured, moulded and even modified by the interests and needs of different groups at different times.

The tradition is 'from the Church, by the Church and for

the Church'. It is not factual data obligingly recorded in 'Q', Mark, 'M' and 'L' for the benefit of the Ph.D. theses of the twentieth century. Mark, no less than 'John', was not written to satisfy the curiosity of distant historians: it was written by and for disciples in order to sustain and evoke faith. This is a different historiography from ours, and we have to face and live with its implications.

Form-analysis seems to establish, then, that the gospel-form itself emerged to give to the proclamation of the primitive Church a literary expression; and that the gospel-material was shaped by and, to some extent, created for the use made of it in that proclamation. It is the third momentous insight given to us by the modern investigation of Christian beginnings.

iii

THE 'JESUS OF HISTORY' AND THE 'HISTORIC CHRIST
IN HIS FULFILMENT'

With these three modern insights, then, we find ourselves questioning Tertullian's paradoxical certainty. Is it certain? And yet, thanks very largely to form-analysis, this is not quite the question we now ask. This is, rather, a nineteenth-century question which the twentieth century seeks to answer by putting it somewhat differently.

The pioneer here was Martin Kähler, professor of theology at Halle where, sixty years ago, he was deeply influencing a student named Paul Tillich. Kähler was one of the first to rebel effectively against that nineteenth-century *Quest of the Historical Jesus* which, whether or not Schweitzer's famous estimate of it was quite fair, was always something of a failure. That quest was critical historicism's honourable attempt to uncover a minimum of reliable facts about the man, Jesus; and to write his life without theological or ecclesiastical presuppositions. It did not reach its goal. Those nineteenth-century lives of Jesus, so far from having the objective disinterestedness of scientific enquiry, tended in fact to be the unconscious expression of the ideas of their authors, who have since been described, therefore, as men looking down a deep well and seeing their own faces

110

at the bottom. Tillich's comment on them was that Christianity is not based on the acceptance of such 'historical novels'.

What, then, is it based on? Kähler's answer was given in a book the (translated) title of which is *The so-called historical Jesus and the historic biblical Christ*. Its title indicates its twofold thesis. It distinguishes, first, between the so-called Jesus of history and the historic Christ. It goes on to argue that this historic Christ is the only object of Christian faith; not an historical Jesus who is and must remain largely inaccessible to us. The only Jesus we know is (to quote a repeated phrase of Kähler's) 'the historic Christ in his fulfilment'; that is, the Christ who is bodied forth in his Church, its on-going life, its worship and fellowship, its sacraments, its preaching and discipline; in short, the risen, living Christ. This, perhaps, is Bultmann's famous distinction between the Proclaimer and the Proclaimed. Indeed, it is the distinction drawn earlier in this century by Benjamin Bacon of Yale. When German scholars were still concerned to work back to an *Ur-Evangelium*, that is, to a supposedly primitive version of the gospel facts, stripped of all later accretions, Bacon reminded them that 'the true *Ur-Evangelium* was nothing written: it was two rites, Baptism and the Supper of the Lord'. Exactly; Christ in his sacramental and eschatological significance for all succeeding generations; Christ in his fulfilment; the Christ to whom the New Testament and the whole Bible become monumental witness. It is the position from which the documents of the New Testament have to be understood in our world. They are unanimous in making a threefold witness. Common to them is the great threefold witness that Jesus in the Christ of God: that his dying was 'for us': that, risen from the dead, he has returned to us, and lives for ever in the fellowship of his redeemed. This is the basic witness, the central affirmation, which is common to New Testament documents from the earliest to the latest. This alone is their original and genuinely common testimony. I am not concerned here with particularities—the mythopoeic build-up of wonder stories which are late rather than early, and marginal rather than central. I am saying that the genuinely unanimous conviction and confession of the New Testament is that this crucified Jesus is the Christ:

that the divine self-disclosure, the divine glory itself, has been realized, once for all, under the empirical conditions of this human life and this human death.

Critical historicism attempted to go behind this unanimous scriptural faith that Jesus in his passion and victory is the Christ of God. If such an attempt be valid—and there are scholars who still think it is—the first three gospels, particularly Mark, are the most important part of the New Testament. But as soon as one realizes that Christian faith has not been and cannot be built on a foundation which historicism is always vainly hoping to excavate, the Epistles and the Fourth Gospel have their own great confessional importance along with that of the Synoptics. There is no essential, *confessional* difference and no ultimate conflict between the differing documents of the New Testament at this focal and decisive point—which is 'the historic Christ in his fulfilment'.

But just how is he fulfilled? In the infallible *magisterium* of an institutional, hierarchical and papal Church? That is one classic answer. In the infallible *magisterium* of sacred Book and evangelical Plan of Salvation? That is another classic answer: the presupposition of every protestant sermon for three centuries, it is now a venerable ruin.

Is he really fulfilled in scholastic orthodoxies; in cut-and-dried legalisms? I cannot think so. That is not what I understand by the historic Christ in his fulfilment.

He is fulfilled where we are aware of him: in the parable of the prodigal; in the Sistine Madonna; in the west front of Bourges Cathedral (something final there, and not to be argued with); in the Office for the Burial of the Dead ('words of such terrible weight'); in John Bunyan; in the Canon of the Mass; in the Byzantine mosaics at Ravenna; in the Society of Friends; in a hymn-tune such as Moab; in Bach's great Sanctus; in the chant of the monks of Camaldoli, high in the cold Apennines, while the world sleeps; in the *Te Deum* ('when Thou hadst overcome the sharpness of death, Thou didst open the kingdom of heaven to all believers'); in Christian lives, quiet, authentic, rare, but a countless host across the centuries; in those words of Romans 8—no more moving words have ever been written—at which the well-worn Bibles of the Scottish crofters always tended to fall open: 'For I am convinced that there is nothing in death or life; in the realm of spirits or superhuman powers; in the world as it is or the world as it shall be; in the forces of the universe; in heights or depths; nothing in all creation that can separate us from the love of God in Christ Jesus our Lord.'

That, surely, is the historic Christ in his fulfilment. That is what font, pulpit and altar declare. That is the beating heart of living faith. It is debtor both to the Jew and to the Greek; both to Athens and to Jerusalem.

SHORT BIBLIOGRAPHY

CORNFORD, F. M. 'A Ritual Basis for Hesiod's Theogony' (in *The Unwritten Philosophy and other Essays*, Cambridge, 1950)

DAVIES, W. D. and DAUBE, D. (editors). *The Background of the New Testament and its Eschatology*, Cambridge, 1955
In the learned essays by many modern scholars here presented to C. H. Dodd, those by Riesenfeld, Schoeps, T. W. Manson, Bornkamm, Clavier, Barrett, Dahl, Ed. Schweizer and A. Wilder are specially relevant for our theme in Chapters V and VI.

DAVIES, W. D. *Christian Origins and Judaism*, Darton, Longman and Todd, 1962

DAUBE, D. *The New Testament and Rabbinic Judaism*, Athlone, 1956

WEISS, J. *Das älteste Evangelium*, Göttingen, 1903

DODD, C. H. *The Parables of the Kingdom*, Nisbet, 1935
—— *New Testament Studies*, Scribners, 1952
No. i, *The Framework of the Gospel Narrative* (1932)
—— *The Interpretation of the Fourth Gospel*, Cambridge, 1953
—— *Historical Tradition in the Fourth Gospel*, Cambridge, 1963

MANSON, T. W. *The Teaching of Jesus*, Cambridge, 1935

JEREMIAS, J. *The Parables of Jesus* (tr. S. H. Hooke), S.C.M., 1954
—— *The Eucharistic Words of Jesus* (tr. A. Ehrhardt), Blackwell, 1955

CREED, J. M. *The Gospel according to St. Luke*, Cambridge, 1930

CAIRD, G. B. *St. Luke* (Pelican Bible Commentaries), 1963

COCHRANE, C. N. *Christianity and Classical Culture*, Oxford, 1940

BLACKMAN, E. C. *Hermeneutics: the Bible as the Vehicle of God's Word to-day* (Canadian Journal of Theology, 1965)

VI

TRADITION AND CRITICISM: THE MEDICINES
OF MODERNITY

THE greatest pioneer in the modern study of the past was
Ranke. 'We meet him at every step', said Lord Acton in
his Inaugural Lecture at Cambridge, 'and he has done
more for us than any other man . . . he stands without a rival.'
Acton went on to speak of Ranke's research and output
throughout seven decades of the nineteenth century. He
wrote seventeen volumes of his Universal History after the age
of eighty-three. We are hardly likely to question Acton's
verdict that it was 'the most astonishing career in Literature'.

Ranke's ideal was an almost inhuman disinterestedness. His
aim as a historian was to repress within himself all romanticism,
patriotism and partisanship: to discover and to state how things
actually happened. A bustling divine who, like him, had
written on the Reformation, once hailed him in Berlin as a
comrade, but Ranke discouraged his advances. 'You', he said,
'are first and foremost a Christian. I am first and foremost a
historian. There is a great difference between us.' It is this
difference between the past as received and the past as investi-
gated, between sacred tradition and scientific historiography,
which must be our concern in this lecture.

i

'THE DEATH OF THE PAST'

The newest of the enduringly divisive issues with which the
ecumenical ideal has to reckon, it nevertheless takes precedence
of them all, since it asks questions about the very basis on which
they are presumed to rest. If the answers to such questions
criticize the received tradition as dubious, or reject it as unhistorical, classic controversies which have always presupposed
it lose their old significance.

For example: the polemic of eighteen centuries over the claims of the Papacy—from Tertullian to the modern Orangeman—has a different basis if the words 'Thou art Peter...', peculiar to Matthew, are deemed by synoptic analysis to be no authentic word of Jesus but one of that Gospel's non-Marcan interpolations, originating in Peter's Antioch as propaganda for its 'favourite son'. That Simon Peter *was* the outstanding member of the earliest group of disciples seems indubitable: but if the logion about Peter as the Rock and as the custodian of the Keys has little more historic credibility than have the wonder-stories about his walking on the sea or his being the chosen one to catch the fish with the silver coin in its mouth, the petrine claims of innumerable papal bulls wither at the root.

Again, in claiming to have rediscovered the apostle Paul and the essential Gospel, classic Protestantism made 'Justification by Faith' its slogan. But if the twentieth-century studies of Deissmann and Schweitzer are right in seeing the famous antithesis of Grace and Works as little more than a subsidiary crater in the wide Pauline volcano, the hostility of Evangelicals towards Catholicism loses something of its traditional motive-power: his 'Christ-mysticism' is more typical of the great Apostle than his epistle to the Galatians.

Again, there is the unending debate about the Christian ministry. In his *Theological Investigations No. VI*, Karl Rahner has recently re-enunciated the traditional Catholic dogma. 'It is theologically certain', he says, 'that the threefold gradation of Bishop, Priest and Deacon is part of the unalterable, divine constitution of the Church.' But the modern scholarship of Bishop Lightfoot and Harnack, of Lietzmann and Canon Streeter—to say nothing of P. N. Harrison's analysis of the Pastorals—demonstrates that what may be pronounced theologically certain is not historically certain; and that this alleged divine constitution of the Church is more probably the result of an explicable human development. The point is that the historians' rejection of the classic hierarchical constitution of the Church before, say, A.D. 150 tends to put out of court the stock controversies of the past about apostolic and episcopal succession.

Again, once the Hebraic and Rabbinical learning of a Dalman, a Manson or a Jeremias has restored to the eucharistic words of Jesus the paschal associations of the Judaism to which they belong, are not the notorious eucharistic controversies of the Christian centuries largely outdated? Is not Transubstantiation itself a museum-piece?

Finally, the source-analysis of the Gospels, from Lachmann to Streeter, is now supplemented, and to some extent superseded, by the form-analysis of a succession of modern scholars from Dibelius to Bultmann. It is an authentic method of research which even theological conservatism does not reject outright. Its proper use has come to stay. Indeed, form-analysis—discussed in the previous chapter—is so eloquent an example not only of the positive value but also of the dangerous negations of historical criticism, that we must consider it a little more closely.

Form-analysis endorses and extends the insight of Wellhausen that the gospels are primarily sources for the history of the early Church that made them; only secondarily are they useful material for determining the course of the life of Jesus. They are products and expressions of the life of the first Christians. The earliest oral tradition about Jesus was floating and plastic; it was shaped and modified by the interests and needs of different groups at different times. As Martin Dibelius insisted, no record of Jesus exists in Christian literature which is free from any editorial or interpretative element. Manifold pressures and redactional influences were at work to give us what is now the canonical witness of the Gospels. The 'Jesus of history' is accessible to us only by this subjective road. There is no other. Jesus himself wrote nothing. Only through the eyes of the first Christians can we see him at all. Just as the analytical comparison of written sources demonstrates how freely Matthew and Luke could deal with their common source Mark, each altering, adding and omitting details; so the first Christian communities used and even manipulated the original oral tradition on occasion. The superb learning of Jeremias has shown this process at work in the Parables. Indeed, it is generally recognized today that much material in the Gospels represents the thought of the Church rather than strictly historical reminiscence. One has only to note the large influence of certain passages in the Prophets and the Psalms on the detailed content of certain gospel narratives, particularly the narrative of the Passion, to realize that the gospel material as we now have it was occasionally built up artificially and even invented for the use to be made of it in the primitive Christian preaching.

Exponents of the technique of form-analysis such as Vincent Taylor, Dodd, Käsemann and Jeremias himself, repudiate excessive scepticism here, of course; the Gospels are not cunningly devised fables. But others such as R. H. Lightfoot, Bultmann and Nineham are less conservative, contending that in no document to which we have access—not even in Mark— is there enough uninterpreted historical material to allow the reconstruction of more than a vague and dubious outline of the history of Jesus. Professor Lightfoot's concluding paragraph has often been quoted: 'For all the inestimable value of the Gospels, they yield us little more than the whisper of his voice; we trace in them but the outskirts of his ways.' That sentence, distressing to many, was later withdrawn by Lightfoot, but he did not withdraw his important and influential book, *History and Interpretation in the Gospels*, to which it was the logical, if too candid, conclusion: he left his analytical research to speak for itself.

This critical agnosticism in which the historical investigation of Christian beginnings can culminate is no isolated pheno-menon today. It has at least three notable ramifications.

The first is the dangerously attractive heresy which would abandon the historical basis of Christianity altogether, sub-stituting for it a mush of vague religiosity. That there was a man of Nazareth in historic time, living, teaching, healing, suffering and dying by crucifixion 'under Pontius Pilate', is a strait waistcoat of actuality which the monist or mystic deep in many of us would sometimes like to be rid of. In certain moods we yearn to indulge what Schleiermacher called 'the sense and taste for the infinite'. André Gide, who found history so uncongenial at school, was thrilled to discover the passage in Schopenhauer which exalts the timelessness of the poet's world over the historian's preoccupation with facts and events, with change and decay:

> That which ne'er and nowhere has befallen,
> That alone it is which cannot age.

Gide revelled in the familiar maxim from Aristotle's *Poetics*; 'philosophy is more important, and poetry is more beautiful, than history'. This attempt to escape from temporal event to eternal changelessness involves the abandonment of a religion rooted in the stuff of history: the emancipating theosophy loses Jesus altogether.

A second development is bound up with modern man's growing sense of his cosmic triviality, as his perspectives of time and space become bewilderingly enlarged. For very many people today this is, consciously or unconsciously, a living issue. The astronomer deep in many of us, newly imaginative about 'space' and about the indisputable possibility of other inhabited worlds, finds it increasingly hard to believe that, in a universe unimaginably ancient and vast, the infinitely small part of it constituted by human history can matter at all. Admittedly there is nothing essentially new in this. When I was an undergraduate it used to be dismissed (a little glibly) as 'astronomical intimidation'. But the Psalmist's question was never more relevant and searching than now: 'When I consider thy heavens, the work of thy fingers, the moon and the stars which thou hast ordained, what is man that thou art mindful of him?' The difficulty is that the Hebraic-Christian understanding of existence does make unique claims for the tiny fragment of time which is human history: it envisages the coming of Christ in terms of the whole cosmos: in him the universe itself is being recreated into a new aeon. But is this eschatological symbolism of prophet and apocalyptist, of 'Colossians' and 'Ephesians', any longer meaningful? Are there rational grounds for taking it more seriously than we now take the crude, sub-Christian phantasies to be found in the middle chapters of the book of Revelation?

A third development has been labelled 'ecclesiological fundamentalism' by Professor Donald Mackinnon of Cambridge, who observes that 'radical scepticism concerning the historical life of Jesus of Nazareth is easily combined with a readiness to accept the historical practices and claims of the Church as self-justifying'. He means that there are theologians who seem happy to concede that no basic historic certainties are attainable with which the developed forms and rites of Catholic tradition may be compared, and by which they may be judged. If most of the alleged facts about the life of Jesus and Christian origins are virtually immune from scrutiny, the sacred tradition (*hagia paradosis*) is all the more unassailable. Mackinnon contends that this type of theology 'issues in an admiring apologetic for actual ecclesiastical institutions. At bottom, of course, it is anti-intellectual; it is also profoundly conservative; in the end identifying what *is* with what *ought* to be; and therefore, of course, it has its peculiar appeal for Anglicans' (*The Listener*, March 23, 1967).

This distinguished Anglican thinker is here warning not only his fellow Anglicans but all of us of the ease with which the wheel can come full circle: form-criticism as a means whereby tradition may retain its old sacrosanctity: historical research as the support of unhistorical structures which it should be demolishing: the acids of modernity, so far from sapping the hoary foundations of ecclesiasticism, ensuring them a longer lease of life. In short, an abuse of the historical method which is as dangerous as it is ironical.

So much, then, for the divisive issues of Tradition and Criticism, and for their various contemporary manifestations.

Forty years ago, in his monograph *The End of Laisser-Faire*, Maynard Keynes made the mordant observation that to suggest social action for the public good to the City of London was like discussing *The Origin of Species* with a bishop sixty years before. 'The first reaction', he wrote, 'is not intellectual but moral: an orthodoxy is in question, and the more persuasive the arguments the graver the offence.'

It was a palpable hit. But much has happened since the twenties. We have all become more Keynesian in outlook (even the City), and less traditional in outlook (even bishops). Indeed, the tension between tradition and modernity has given to our inherited ecclesiological divisions a new complexity. Once neatly vertical, they now tend to be stratified horizontally in addition, the result being a chessboard where movement is irregular and unpredictable. Bishops have always been able to incline to left or right, backwards or forwards; but now the pawns seem equally mobile. I, for instance, am a Protestant, yet my sense of kinship with a Duchesne or a Von Hügel is much keener than it is with a member of the Sovereign Grace Union or a Billy Graham. Though I am a convinced Free Churchman, conscious of differing in no way that matters from Ernest Payne, I am nevertheless nearer in mind and heart to Bishop Huddleston than I am to the (white) Baptists of Arkansas. I have more in common, too, with Myrna Hooker and J. A. T. Robinson than I have with the British and Foreign Bible Society; and it would seem certain that the Lutheran Paul Tillich, to whom I owe much, was closer to Bishop Huddleston than I am to the (white) Baptists of Synod.

This change is due in part to non-theological factors, but in the main to that triumphant critical historiography which Professor H. J. Plumb has surveyed in his lectures entitled *The Death of the Past*. My point here is that the lively critical historicism of our time is providing new opportunities for ecumenical action, and that modernity is not necessarily and not always corrosive acid. It can and should be healing medicine. What, then, is the prescription for its make-up and its effective use? I offer an answer under three heads.

ii

B.C. AND A.D.: REVELATION ACTUALIZED AND RECEIVED IN HISTORIC EVENT

First: the essential Christian Gospel affirms divine redemption, actualized and received in the stuff of history.

What is Christianity? The letters B.C. and A.D. are our first clue. They indicate an Event in which the old era ends and the new begins. 'Christianity was born', says Tillich, 'not with the birth of the man who is called Jesus but in the moment when one of his followers was driven to say to him "Thou art the Christ".' Tillich means, presumably, not only that the essential revelation is strictly historical and not a legendary idyll; but also that this historic Event on which Christianity is based has two aspects: the fact of the Man of Nazareth, and the reception of this fact by those who believed on him as the Christ, and lived a new life in him. In the earliest tradition the first of those who so received him was Simon Peter. His momentous confession stands at the centre of that tradition, as preserved in Mark's Gospel. Christianity begins neither at Bethlehem nor at Nazareth but at Caesarea Philippi with the words 'Thou art the Christ'. The words 'Thou art Peter . . .', etc., interpolated at this point in Matthew's Gospel, are a later intrusion. The historic basis of the Church is the confession to which Peter gave representative utterance. Origen's exegetical comment, '*ginometha Petros*' ('we are Peter'), is right, since Peter speaks here for us all.

But there is something more, of course. This Event at Caesarea Philippi—this point in history where B.C. becomes A.D.—is the momentous turning-point in Mark's narrative because, while the words 'Thou art the Christ' are still sounding in the reader's ears, he is made aware that the Christ has to die. Implicit in the very acceptance by Jesus of this Messianic title is his rejection by the principalities and powers of this world. As the Christ he brings the new age of salvation by participating completely in man's immemorial predicament. He subjects himself to the conditions of our existence and all that they involve of woe and death; triumphing over them. He dies our death victoriously. In him, man's estrangement—from himself, from his neighbour and from God—is overcome.

Our religion knows and preaches this as Salvation. It was preached, for example in Forsyth's memorable address to the Congregational Union, sixty-five years ago. Because the closing passage included words which precisely illustrate the three truths which I am emphasizing in this chapter, I quote from them:

> . . . I read the story of the father who beseeches Christ to heal his son. I hear the answer of the Lord 'I will come down and heal him'. 'Him'. That means me. The words are life to my distempered soul. . . . They come with a promise here and now. I

see the heavens open and the Redeemer at the right hand of God. I hear a great voice from heaven, and these words are the words of the Saviour himself to me, 'I will come down and heal him'. And upon them he rises from his eternal throne; he takes his way through a ready lane of angels, archangels, the high heavenly host and the glorious fellowship of saints. They part at his coming for they know where he would go. . . . He moves from the midst of complete obedience, spiritual love, holy intelligence, ceaseless worship and perfect praise. He is restless amid all that, in search of me,—me sick, falling, lost, despicable, desperate. He comes, he finds, he heals me on the wings of these words. I do not ask the critics for assurance that the incident took place exactly as recorded. I will talk of that when I am healed. It is a question for those who are trying to frame a biography of Jesus, or discussing the matter of miracles. It has brought to dying me the life of Christ. . . . For me these words are more than historical; they are sacramental. They carry not a historic incident, merely, but the historic Gospel.

Exactly. The essential Christian Gospel affirms redemption actualized and received in the stuff of history. But Forsyth's honest recognition of the witness of the critics, and his percipient anticipation of something like form-analysis back there in 1905, begin to disclose the second truth which I wish to emphasize. Forsyth did not evade it, nor did he soft-pedal it. He was not unaware that critical scholarship may and does take 'ego elthōn therapeuso auton' as aorist subjunctive rather than future indicative, the probable translation being 'Am I to come and heal him?' It is a translation supported by the closely parallel story of the Syro-Phoenician woman where the initial unwillingness of Jesus to heal is overcome by the woman's apt reply. Forsyth knew, too, that there is actually no suggestion of coming *down* to heal in this story of the Centurion's son: the authority for his addition of this word was Philippians 2, and obvious passages in the Fourth Gospel. But such considerations do not invalidate what Forsyth was saying: they did not prevent his hearing and receiving and proclaiming that essential Gospel of our redemption which is writ large in the New Testament.

EXISTENTIAL FAITH AND HONEST HISTORICAL JUDGMENT

This brings us, then, to our second truth: that this affirmation is completely compatible with uncompromising historical honesty.

Let us admit, in passing, that historical honesty is an ideal to which we rarely, if ever, attain. Here, Ranke has to be qualified by Freud. Complete impartiality is not attainable at the drop of a hat. The confident appeal to the bar of history, as though this were as straightforward as verifying a quotation in a book, is now seen to be a little naïve. The claim to be completely unprejudiced is itself prejudice. More is now known about the way in which the historian's unconscious presuppositions affect his interpretation of available evidence. As no empirical description of an historical figure is ever without its subjective elements, the bar of history can turn out to be an arena of rival jurisdictions. Our appeal to it, therefore, is less confident than it was. When we have done our best, our work will still be tentative and provisional. All history has to be corrected by more history—the Whigs by Butterfield; Motley by Geyl; Glover by Momigliano. Professor Plumb is well aware that he will be superseded in due course.

But having admitted that scientific historiography is not necessarily infallible because its intentions are honest, we must add that it is nevertheless indispensable, especially in the field of biblical research where it is still so suspect. To those who are temperamentally prone to tremble for the Ark, biblical research is always suspect because it appears to criticize not only the sources called Gospels but also the revelation which they contain. The Christian revelation being actualized in historical event, can its revelatory content be separated from its form as historical report? Doesn't your critical historicism undercut faith itself? The very designation of the corpus of Christian scripture as 'Holy' scripture seems to give validity to this fear. Hands off the Bible!

We have already noticed the relative failure of attempts to 'uncover' a life of Jesus of Nazareth which would be solely empirical and biographical. There is no original picture which scientific processes of restoration might give back to us. Such analogies are misleading. The only reports about Jesus which we have are reports of him as the Christ. The point which Forsyth makes in passing is that certitude of faith does not imply certitude about detailed questions of historical research. Tillich endorses this. 'The role of faith', he says, 'is existential; it concerns the totality of our being. Historical judgments are theoretical; they are open to constant and continuing criticism.' In short, the literary form called 'gospel' is a *portrait* of the Man who is seen and acknowledged to be the Christ. Not every single, isolated feature of this portrait can be verified and guaranteed with historical certainty; but through the portrait as a whole—set, as we shall see, in its frame of christological symbolism—the new life of salvation is mediated. Forsyth was testifying, not only for himself but for all of us, when he described the portrait as sacramental. The actual, personal life encountered by the first disciples created the portrait: it is still the medium of redeeming power. Faith does not guarantee all the factual details of the concrete biblical material: it guarantees the material as the sacramental portrayal and conveyance of the saving power in him who is the Christ.

iv

MYTH AND SYMBOL: THE DISTORTIONS OF LITERALISM

But now for the third truth: this affirmation refuses to be limited to the factual. Presented apart from its proper mythology and proven symbolism, it is misrepresented.

Theology owes much to the insights of modern research into the great christological symbols of the Bible, derived and developed as they are from their Semitic, Persian or Hellenic environment in the ancient world of the near East: Son of Man, Man from heaven, Messiah, Son of God, Lord, Logos. We have been taught to distinguish the successive phases of their historical development from their respective cultural and religious origins to their transformation and use by Christianity as interpretations of the event on which it is based. In the New Testament we see them being baptized into Christ. That they have been and still are distorted by literalism and popular superstition is a depressing fact; but it in no way detracts from their true function and meaning as powerful symbols: statements of what cannot be literally stated without distortion. No one who listened to Forsyth in that assembly of 1905 supposed that his imagery of the Saviour's descent from high heaven was to be taken literally. Yet that is the danger with which religious language is always being threatened. Evidence of this is given in Tillich's systematic analysis of the development of each of these symbols, through successive stages, to a final stage of threatening crudity. He says, for example, of the much-discussed title 'Son of Man': 'Literalism takes the fourth step by imagining a transcendent Being who, once upon a time, was sent down from his heavenly place and transmuted into a man. In this way, a true and powerful symbol becomes an absurd story, and the Christ becomes a half-God, a particular being between God and man.' To put this in another way, heresies such as this heresy of Arianism (for that is what it virtually is) are discovered or invented by the literalist in the New Testament itself. Heresies are often potential distortions which time has made actual and evident.

This is well illustrated by the symbolism, not of 'coming down' but of 'going up'. What of the popular theology of the Ascension? Is its spatial symbolism to be taken literally? Obviously not. We have already noticed that Calvin repudiated the Lutheran view that the glorified body of the ascended Christ is everywhere and that his seat at God's right hand is illocal. He insisted on retaining the old Augustinian concept that the body of Christ is in heaven. But Calvin explains, of course, that he is not thinking *mathematice vel localiter* (in terms of the mathematics of space) when so expressing himself. 'What!' he exclaims. 'Are we supposed to locate Christ amid the spheres, or do we build a hut for him among the planets (*tugurium ei exstruimus inter planetas*)? Heaven, where Christ is, is God's glorious dwelling-place (*magnificum palatium dei*) transcending the totality of the cosmos itself.' In short, Christ's seat at God's right hand is not to be taken literally: it means that he reigns as living Lord in all the might, majesty and glory of the Father.

Those who profess belief in the Ascension as the movement

of a physical, tangible body from the surface of our planet into space have to meet J. A. T. Robinson's question: 'Do you really think it went on through space, passing out of the gravitational pull, first of the earth, then of the sun; and that now after two thousand light-years it is somewhere in the middle of the Milky Way?' No one does think like this, of course. But, as Robinson observes, this only shows how lazy much of our thinking is.

Robinson is here deliteralizing a New Testament story. Is this, in principle, anything new? The Fourth Gospel initiated this process of reinterpretation nearly nineteen centuries ago. But he goes on to say something so surprising and instructive to many people that it should be quoted:

> We have all been brought up to the idea that the Ascension is a separate historical event which happened forty days after Easter. But a study of the New Testament shows that this is entirely St. Luke's construction. Indeed, it is only in his second volume, *Acts*, that we find the familiar schema: the Resurrection, followed forty days later by the Ascension, and ten days after that by the gift of the Spirit. In St. John all three take place on Easter Day and are part of a single complex. In fact, right through the rest of the New Testament (including St. Luke's own Gospel) and well on after it, until the book of *Acts* becomes regarded as scripture, the exaltation of Jesus is regularly linked with Easter. The Resurrection appearances are of a Christ who, as he says on the Emmaus road, has *already* entered into his glory.

Robinson adds that, as the father of the Christian Year, the author of *Acts* has

> ... pegged out these different aspects of Easter along a line of time, placing one after three days, another after the symbolic biblical interval of forty days, attaching yet another to the liturgical feast of Pentecost.
>
> (J. A. T. Robinson: *But that I can't believe*, Fontana, 1968)

The ecumenical relevance of this stimulating example of what modern bible-study could and should be is that multitudes of modern Christians in all branches of the Church are in entire accord with theologians so representatively diverse as

Forsyth, Tillich and Robinson in treasuring the mythological symbolism of the New Testament while disavowing the crude distortions to which it can give rise. Here there is wide common ground on which they find themselves standing together. It is modernity which could do much to heal some of our traditional divisions.

Such opportunities, however, are offset by our inherited difficulties. It has been a theological cliché of our time that Christianity is rooted in history: our faith is founded on the rock of historic happening. But if this be taken to mean faith in certain events as *credenda* rather than faith as personal trust in Jesus as the Christ, this truth can involve two dangers. One is that critical questions as to Christian origins may be regarded by believers as a threat to faith; and obscurantism will masquerade as orthodoxy. The other is that non-Christians may think that they have only to expose dubieties in Christianity's historic origins to destroy its credibility as religion.

The stories about the birth of Jesus illustrate the dilemma. When Burne-Jones was at work on a picture of the Annunciation a girl asked him whether the story is true. 'It is too beautiful not to be true' was his unsatisfactory reply. But there was more to the reply than the romantic idealism of his generation. The story of the virginal conception may indeed assure us of what we need and long to know, namely that our salvation comes into our history rather than out of it: that the Redeemer *is* the Man from *heaven*: that his coming, independent of the chances and changes of man's mortal life, is dependent on God alone: Glory to God in the highest. It is surely fitting that he who is to be the bearer of the new life of the new age is predestined and announced, so to speak, in his very birth. The Christian heart responds to the intention of such a belief with ecstatic agreement.

But as historical evidence the birth-stories are exceedingly fragile. The earliest Gospel, Mark, knows nothing of them. They appear about eighty years after the events which they purport to describe. Paul, the author of the earliest documents in the New Testament and the first Christian man whom we know indubitably as a fully real historical figure, says not a word about them. The fourth evangelist, writing probably at the turn of the century, ignores them; indeed, by implication, he rejects them; like Paul, he uses other, more stupendous categories of interpretation. Most New Testament scholars conclude that the opening chapters of Matthew and Luke are idyll rather than history. The story of Mary's virginal conception belongs to the mythological framework of the Scriptures. Moreover, Burne-Jones was more wrong than right if his answer meant that he did not discern how dangerous the beautiful Christmas story can be to the truth of the Gospel. I am not thinking here of the cult of the Virgin Mary which is distinctive of Catholic rather than of Protestant piety, but of the tendency common to both which unites them. All Christians tend to qualify the completeness of the Christological paradox in the moment of confessing it. The Christ is 'very Man' as well as 'very God', yet the participation of a human father in his procreation, which would make him 'in all points like as we are', is disallowed. The Christmas story reinforces that docetic and monophysite tendency which we have seen to be rarely absent from Christian piety and even from Christian thought. It is itself an important step in that direction, for it anticipates the impersonal human nature of the Chalcedonian formula and the 'Apollinarian' tendencies in the christology of the 'graecizing Westerns' and of Luther. It is one of several ways in which Protestants as well as Catholics betray a pious reluctance to let the Incarnation be complete, the Christ participating fully in the human predicament.

This issue is one of many raised by the modern biblical research which has been our theme in this chapter. It may serve to illustrate the fact that just because our much-translated Bible is inexpressibly precious to us, it is now far less in need of translation than of interpretation.

SHORT BIBLIOGRAPHY

CULLMANN, O. *Peter*, S.C.M., 1953
PLUMB, J. H. *The Death of the Past*, Macmillan, 1969
MACKINNON, D. *The Stripping of the Altars*, London, 1969

LIGHTFOOT, R. H. *History and Interpretation in the Gospels*, Bamptons, 1934

PERRIN, N. *Rediscovering the Teaching of Jesus*, S.C.M., 1967

NINEHAM, D. E. (editor). *Studies in the Gospels*, Oxford

DAVIES, W. D. *Reflections on a Scandinavian approach to the Gospel Tradition (Neotestamentica et Patristica*, Leiden, 1962)

―― *The Setting of the Sermon on the Mount*, Cambridge, 1964

BARRETT, C. K. *Jesus and the Gospel Tradition*, S.P.C.K., 1967

TILLICH, P. *Journal of Liberal Religion*, II, 13–33, 1940

―― *Systematic Theology*, vol. II, Chicago, 1957

ROBINSON, J. A. T. *But that I can't believe*, Fontana, 1968

DEWART, L. *The Future of Belief*, Burns Oates, 1967

―― *The Foundations of Belief*, Burns Oates, 1970

BEVAN, E. *Symbolism and Belief*, Beacon, 1938

GOODENOUGH, E. R. *Jewish Symbols in the Graeco-Roman world*, vols. III and IV (Bollingen Series, XXXVII)

BUONAIUTI, E. *Pellegrino di Roma*, Laterza, 1964

VII

EPILOGUE: THREE ECUMENICAL TALKING-POINTS

THIS survey has been largely concerned with the historic background to those divisions among Christians which are the enduring measure of the ecumenical problem. It has sought to be realistic as well as eirenical, explicit rather than evasive. Of the talking-points which emerge three seem to be pre-eminent and formidable; and of these the one which is 'one and all alone' is what Professor Plumb has called 'the death of the past'. In the acids of modernity the strife and divisions of Christendom are offered healing medicine. The ecumenical movement faces no more crucial issue than this, in the long run.

i

'THE MAN IN BLACK' IN THE PUBLIC HOUSE

Along with the steady erosion of the dogmatic structures of the classic past in our modern world, and the disruption of the old modes of piety, there goes a growing scepticism as to the reliability of what is ostensibly historical evidence in the New Testament. The theological iconoclasm of the past hundred years is its own evidence. Medieval *Summa* and protestant *Confession* are now museum pieces because their use of Scripture is completely out of date. Reading the Bible 'in the flat', and solving the mystery of existence with the arbitrary citation of 'proof texts', is an absurd caricature of the proper use of such foundation documents. So used, the Bible is abused. The immediate relevance of the criticism and form-analysis which we were considering in the previous chapter is that distinctive and divisive claims made by the Churches often rest on textual proof which can no longer authenticate itself as such.

These critical issues are commonplaces of the study but they are too rarely allowed recognition in pulpit, religious journal or

Bible-study group. Sooner or later, however, they will make their break-through, causing some of the ecclesiological and credal battles of our schismatic past to look as archaic as the joustings in a medieval tilt-yard.

Further, such issues are not the preserve of specialists. Cautious or timorous silence about them is not only un-justifiable but dangerous. Borrow's Lavengro complained that the Man in Black denied in the public house what he admitted in the dingle. The ecumenical movement will owe much to modern men in black when they succeed in narrowing the gap between dingle and public house, and in making their learning popular (in the best sense of that ambiguous word). The continuing use of the Bible for sustaining the very life of the Church is not dependent on the maintenance of obsolete and untrue notions as to its character and meaning.

ii

THE RELATIVITIES OF HISTORY: IS ANY CHURCH ORDER ABSOLUTE?

The second issue, which has long been a notoriously divisive one, is that of Church Order: whether any such order is solely authoritative because ordained by God; or whether, as W. D. Davies has shown, or as in Canon Streeter's classic discussion, there existed no single type of Church Order in New Testament times; so that, in the words of *Alice in Wonderland* 'Everyone has won, and all shall receive prizes'. As British Baptists recently asked in formal assembly: is the absence of structural unity a major sin in the life of the Church Universal? It may be doubted. Yet some credal and institutional form is surely indispensable as a minimum acknowledgment of what the Gospel is, in all its objective 'givenness'; and as an attempt, while avoiding legalism, to guarantee that another gospel shall not be substituted for it. No Independent, whether Baptist or Congregationalist, advocates anarchy in order to vindicate the precious principle of spiritual liberty.

But can there be logical concord between those who still insist that this Gospel is expressed and conveyed only through priestly and hierarchical order (anything else being bogus and illusory) and those whose tradition and personal experience make such claims irrelevant and even perverse? In the New Testament, just as no individual Christian is ever called a 'saint', so none is ever called a 'priest'. These features of Catholic life and order emerge much later. Is it not verifiable fact, humanly speaking, that the Spirit sometimes uses Catholic order as its channel and sometimes does not? How, otherwise, are we to understand not only our own mothers, and 'devout women not a few', but also a Bunyan, a Charles Wesley or an Alexander Whyte? It is now politely conceded that such non-catholics represent 'uncovenanted mercies'. But if this were so, their very extent across the centuries and the continents would make the word 'uncovenanted' meaningless. Was Canon Lacey right when he pronounced St. Paul's apostolate 'a very dangerous exception' or was he being just absurd?

A further point here was made by Professor C. K. Barrett in his instructive Shaffer Lectures. Criticizing Gerhardsson's 'picture of an apostolic college situated in Jerusalem, studying the sacred tradition, and issuing on the basis of it authorized interpretations, exegesis of Old Testament scripture, and rules for the government of church life', Barrett observes that

> . . . this is not a convincing account of the facts. We have no precise knowledge of what the Apostles did in Jerusalem. Luke, writing towards the end of the first century, and evidently on the basis of very scanty knowledge, does his best to represent the Twelve as an impressive central body, but he tells us nothing of what they did, can only associate them with a few incidents he is able to report concerning Peter and John, and even so soon loses interest in them.
>
> (*Jesus and the Gospel Tradition*, 1967, pp. 10–11)

For well over eighteen centuries Christian tradition has been using the word 'apostolic' and the number 'twelve' as a sacred spell or bemusing enchantment to give credibility and authority to its statements and claims about Christian origins; whereas in fact we know very little about the Twelve in comparison with what we know about Lacey's 'very dangerous exception'—the real apostolic founder of the Church in the Roman world and the effective agent of its expansion there.

133

THE INCARNATION AND THE 'SECULAR'

Our third important talking-point may be covered by the fashionable word 'secular'. The ecumenical ideal has large secular implications of which no Church is yet fully aware. *Oikoumene* means the inhabited world; that is, the whole world, all mankind; and the true ecumenical society is the unlimited community, that ultimate, universal and ideal society of human dreams in comparison with which our empirical ecclesiasticism is always a saddening caricature. The churches are so ecclesiastical, their ecclesiasticism so clerical and their clericalism so male, that their essential genius often appears exclusive rather than inclusive: relatively few of them have yet moved beyond the bland male assumption of the good Oecolampadius in his oration to the clergy of Basle in 1530, that church discipline cannot be put into the hands of the Congregation since it contains women and children (Rupp, *op. cit.* p. 39.)

The same excluding principle affects even the ecumenical activities of the Churches. Are they not preoccupied with themselves even when busy about schemes for losing themselves in a larger unity? Are they not turned inward upon themselves rather than genuinely involved in the common life of mankind? Thomas Carlyle's splenetic description of the Methodism of his day, 'with its eye ever upon its own navel', is really a criticism of us all. Indeed, if we are to be just to John Wesley himself, we may not forget that it was he who declared 'the world is my parish'. There is a true sense in which the *world* is the Church which God loved, which Christ purchased and which the Holy Ghost sanctifies: not our several cherished ecclesiastical establishments. Commenting on the sentence in the *Areopagitica*, 'God is decreeing to begin some new and great period in his church', Dr. Christopher Hill observes: 'The last three words convey to a modern reader something quite different from what Milton intended. "God's church" was for him roughly what we mean by "mankind", "humanity". Milton was certainly not referring to one church among many . . . he was referring to all mankind, though no doubt to the elect in particular.'

At the Synod of Dort, three and a half centuries ago, John Hales of Eton listened to Episcopius as he expounded the words 'God so loved the world'. Deeply moved, he went back to his lodging and wrote in his Journal 'I bade John Calvin "Good night".' That fragment of the history of our unhappy divisions is no adequate appraisal of either Calvinism or Arminianism, of course; but it vindicates the universality of the Gospel and it can still illustrate the widespread modern demand that the religion of Jesus as the Christ be true to its own genius: that it be truly and effectively and universally secular, as alone befits the Gospel of the Word made Flesh.

SHORT BIBLIOGRAPHY

BARRETT, C. K. *op. cit.* p. 130 above
DAVIES, W. D. *Christian Origins and Judaism*
   No. ix, *A Normative Pattern of Church Life in the New Testament?*
   No. x, *Light on the Ministry in the New Testament*
LITTELL, F. H. *The Anabaptist View of the Church*, Boston, 1958
HILL, C. *God's Englishman: Oliver Cromwell and the English Revolution*, London, 1970
SMITH, R. G. *Secular Christianity*, Collins, 1966
BETHGE, E. *Dietrich Bonhöffer: A Biography*, Collins, 1970
ST. PIERRE, M. DE. *Les Nouveaux Prêtres*, La Table Ronde, 1964
SILONE, I. *Vino e Pane*, Mondadori, 1955
—— *Uscita di Sicurezza*, Valecchi, 1969

INDEX

absurditas, 59, 63
'absurdity of Christianity', 37f
Acton, Lord, 29, 115
Alexandria and Antioch, 19, 61f
Anabaptism, 29f, 32, 46
Anselm, 42
Apollinaris, 65, 67, 129
Apostolic Constitutions, 15
Apostolicae curae, 19
Aquinas, 35, 57, 85, 97
Areopagitica, 134
Aristotle, 37, 97
Ascension, The, 78f, 126f
Athanasius contra mundum, 21
Augustine: his ecclesiology, 17ff;
  his two-sidedness, 22f, 28; on
  predestination, 22f; on corpus
  permixtum, 29; on church and
  state, 31; on the Eucharist,
  45f, 80; as 'bridge', 68
Aulén, G., 42f

Bacon, B., 111
Barrett, C. K., 9, 133
Barry, Bishop, 19
Barth, K., 22, 49, 98f
Bartlet, V., 16
Berengar, 53, 72
'Blues and Greens', 19
Bonhöffer, D., 56
Brenz, 72
Browne, R., 7
Bucer, 45, 47

Bunyan, 112, 133
Burkitt, F. C., 41
Burne-Jones, E. C., 128

Caesarea Philippi, 122
Calvin: his debt to Augustine,
  22, 23f, 80; his ecclesiology,
  23f, 28; his attack on medievalism, 44, 73; his classic Protestantism, 44–49; his catholic
  orthodoxy, 53, 89, 92; his
  concept of 'substance', 76f;
  his eucharistic theology, 75–
  92; the Spirit as 'channel',
  86f; the 'medicine of immortality', 92f; the Ascension,
  126; his achievement, 88f
Canon of the Mass, 41
'Capernaite', 53
Carlyle, T., 134
Carter, H. C., 56, 60
Cassian, J., 22
Cathari, 29
Catholicism, distinctive claim
  of, 25
Chalcedon, 61
Christology, patristic and credal,
  60ff; monophysite, 64ff; Lutheran and Reformed, 60,
  62f, 72, 81f
Church, conceptions of the; Old
  Catholic, 12–16; Medieval,
  18–24; Protestant, 25–29; as

137